The Grub Wrangler and Gruff Dog Biscuit Almanac

The Grub Wrangler and Gruff Dog Biscuit Almanac

Chrissy Hartmann

Prickle Forrest Books
Published in Wooster, OH USA

Copyright

chrissyhartmann@sssnet.com

Disclaimer:

The content of this book is for informational purposes only and is not intended as veterinary advice. Always consult a licensed veterinarian before introducing new foods or treats into your dog's diet, especially if your dog has allergies, health conditions, or specific dietary requirements. The author and publisher are not responsible for any adverse effects or outcomes that may result from the use of the recipes or guidance contained herein.

Publisher: Prickle Forrest Books

Library of Congress Control Number: 2025922498

Published in Wooster, Ohio, USA

ISBN Paperback: 978-1-965780-11-4

ISBN Digital: 978-1-965780-14-5

Cover Design: Getcovers

Editors: Cary Harter

Alexandra Musselman

First Edition: November 2025

www.chrissyhartmann.com

Dedication

To the *Mairs Veterinary Clinic*, specifically my grandpa, “Doc,” Robert E. Mairs, my “Uncle Doc,” Robert F. Mairs, and my cousin, Richard A. Mairs, all vets who have won the hearts of many dog and cat owners here in my little neck of the woods. Thank you for your dedication and love to our furry friends.

Special Thanks...

I'd like to thank with hugs and kisses the HartFelt Boarding Kennels who without their expertise and photos this almanac of dog biscuits and more would have never hit the trails.

The Grub Wrangler and I don't just like HartFelt Boarding Kennels — We trust them like an old trail horse that never lets you down. Out here, trust is earned by showing up day after day, rain or shine, and that's exactly what the HartFelt crew does. They treat every pup that trots through their gate like one of their own, making sure each tail gets its fair share of wags and belly rubs. As the resident grub wrangler likes to say with a half-smile, "Ain't no dog leaves here without a full belly, a clean coat, and a happy heart."

From sunrise to sundown, the folks at HartFelt pour their hearts into caring for every four-legged guest. Whether it's luxury boarding, daycare full of romp and play, or a gentle grooming session that leaves a pup looking sharp, they do it with the kind of attention that only comes from genuine love. "These dogs ain't just boarders," the grub wrangler grumbles while refilling a water bowl, "they're part of the family — even the ones that drool more than they should." And that's the spirit we appreciate most. HartFelt isn't just a kennel; it's a home away from home, built on thirty years of care, trust, and a whole lot of heart.

And just so you know more about what I'm jawing about, I'll let it come straight from the horse's mouth, so contact them. Cause they're a friendly crew who love to talk pets.

HartFelt Boarding Kennels
6187 Township Rd 219,
Big Prairie, OH 44611

(330) 674-0240

Info@hartfeltkennels.com
https://hartfeltkennels.com/

Contents

Acknowledgments

They say it takes a whole herd to raise a pup, and I reckon the same holds true for a dog biscuit almanac. This book sure didn't come together on its own, and I've got my own herd of folks to thank for helping me along the way.

First off, to my grandparents — the ones who taught me how to love a critter proper. You showed me that pets aren't just animals — they're family. I still carry those early lessons in kindness every time I scratch a pup behind the ears or sneak a treat to a barn cat.

To HartFelt Boarding Kennel, especially the head groomer, Mary Hartmann who opened the doors and shared her know-how — bless you for your patience, your humor, and your deep understanding of what makes a dog truly happy. You reminded me that wagging tails and clean paws are made of equal parts skill and heart.

To my family and friends and their four-legged sidekicks, thank you for the stories, the slobber, and the snapshots. Every goofy grin and muddy pawprint added real joy to these pages.

A tip of the hat to my director of photography — Jacob Benchoff — bless your heart for putting up with me every time I say, *"Just one more picture."* We both know that's a lie. Your eye for detail and your easy laugh brought this book to life.

To my husband, who rides shotgun through every bit of my creative chaos — thank you for humoring my wild ideas and for loving me through all the biscuit testing, flour clouds, and late-night writing marathons.

To my editors, Cary Harter and Alexandra Musselman who keeps my words wrangled and my commas corralled — your steady hand and sharp eye turned these rough notes into something worth reading.

And most of all, to God — for the gift of words, for the love He plants in our hearts, and for every pawprint that leaves a mark on my life.

This one's for all the folks who believe that a little oat flour, a lot of love, and one good dog... or cat can make any day better.

Chrissy Hartmann

Chapter 1 Introduction

So, you're ready for a ruff and ready western grub guide for dogs and a few cats too?
Well partner, you've found the right book then.

Now, I'll admit it right up front—I'm a contemporary western romance author. I usually spend my days wrangling grumpy cowboys and stubborn heroines, not chasing down chuckwagon tales about a cook and his dog. But The Grub Wrangler and his partner, Gruff, had other ideas.

From the time Gruff tumbled into camp as a clumsy pup to the years he strutted around like he owned the chuckwagon, that dog lived a story worth sharing. Along the trail, The Grub Wrangler figured out that supper didn't just belong to the cowboys – Gruff deserved a plate too. And that's how some downright tasty, healthy treats came to be.

Now, Gruff tells me I ought to hurry up and get these stories written because, in his words, "a dog's patience only stretches as far as his stomach."

Fair enough. I've had cats and dogs underfoot my whole life, and with a great grandpa, grandpa, uncle, and cousin who all pulled veterinarian duty, I like to think I know a wee thing or two about critters.

So, bear with me – romance may be my usual trail, but this time, I'm just the scribe for a dog with a belly full of stories and a chuckwagon cook who kept him fed.

This cookbook was born from years of caring for dogs through every stage of life. Whether raising a curious pup, keeping a prime-time herder sharp, or comforting an old-timer, the recipes and care tips here will help nourish your loyal companion. With a western twist, practical guidance, and notes from our Grub Wrangler... and Gruff.

This guide aims to be your sidekick on the trail of dog care.

1.1 Go Natural

Well now, if you've stumbled onto this here dog biscuit almanac, you've figured out one thing right off: these ain't no run-of-the-mill, store-bought knick-knacks for your critter. Naw — you're dealing with real-deal all-natural ingredients. We're talking:

Pumpkin

Sweet potatoes

Vitamin E (that's good for their immune system, don't ya know)

Fish oil (for that slick coat)

Oats

Peanut butter (Xylitol free)

Ginger

Salmon

... And plenty more good-for-them stuff you can dig up between the covers of this here cookbook.

Sure, you could mosey down to the store and snag some biscuits — or hell, chuck them table scraps.

But let me tell ya straight: that won't do for your four-legged barn buddy. Those factory-made snacks won't give them none of the wholesome nutrients packed into these homemade morsels.

Now I know what you're thinking Grub Wrangler, my purse strings are tighter than a cow's rear end, and I got no spare minute after wrestling cattle. Fine. I'll give ya that. But ask yourself — when was the last time you'd choke down cardboard for supper, just so your belly wouldn't grumble?

Your best friend — be it pup or kitten — sure as shooting deserves better than cardboard. You feed them right, you get loyalty and good health in return. They're not just pets — they're partners out here under sky. And who wouldn't want their partner around for a good long spell?

Top Ten Reasons to Make Your Own Dog Biscuits

1. Simple as dirt — these biscuits don't demand fancy ingredients. You'll likely have most already.

2. All-natural goodness—nothing artificial to mess up their insides.

3. Better nutrition — real pumpkin, salmon, oats, and vitamins beat whatever's in mass-market treats.

4. Customizable — got a pup with allergies, or just picky? You control what goes in.

5. Freshness counts — no stale factory loaf; these come straight from your oven, still warm.

6. Cost control — yeah, homesteading costs more time, but the quality more than pays for itself.

7. Bonding activity — you're making them with your own hands and more than likely while they watch. That counts for something.

8. Smells like home — no mystery chemicals. Just real smells that say "I care."

9. Healthier treats — fiber from sweet potato and oats helps digestion, fish oil and vitamin E help coats shine.

10. It's your call—you pick the ingredients, the quantity, the frequency—no dog food giants calling the shots.

So, if you've got a lick of grit left after the day's worth of wrangling, keep reading and bake them up. Your pup will appreciate it — and you'll sleep better knowing you didn't feed them nothing less than the best.

— The Grub Wrangler

1.2 Trail Warning for Pet Lovers

Now listen up, folks — before you go rustling up any of these recipes for your pup, keep a sharp eye on the ingredients. These treats are made from nothing but natural goodness, the kind The Grub Wrangler himself would serve up with pride. But every dog's different, and what sits fine with one belly might not sit so well with another.

Always check with your veterinarian first, especially if your pup's taking any medicine that might tangle with certain foods.

And remember, dogs will gobble down just about anything you set in front of them — even when their bodies are hollering don't do it.

So, take it slow when trying out new treats, keep the portions small to start, and make sure your best friend stays healthy, happy, and ready for the next adventure on the trail – or on the couch.

Now, Gruff's got a word or two to add:
Howdy, folks! Let me just say, I'm all for you taking this caution business to heart–means I get to stick around longer and sample more of these fine vittles. So don't go feeding me something my belly can't handle, or we'll both regret it. Trust me, I've tried eating boots, rocks, and one unfortunate fence post. None of them ended well. Stick with these recipes, use a little common sense, and I'll wag my tail, lick your hand, and happily volunteer for seconds. And thirds. And, well, you get the idea.

Now on the serious side, I've wrangled a list of harmful Foods & Their Side Effects along with who to contact for help so keep reading then dog ear these pages in case you need to find them right quick.

1.3 Harmful Foods

1. Chocolate
— Contains theobromine and caffeine. Causes vomiting, diarrhea, rapid heart rate, tremors, seizures, arrhythmias, internal bleeding, and possibly death.

2. Grapes & Raisins
— Can trigger acute kidney failure. Symptoms include vomiting, diarrhea, lethargy, increased drinking and urination, abdominal pain, dehydration, and kidney dysfunction.

3. Peanut Butter Containing Xylitol
— Leads to rapid insulin release, causing hypoglycemia, seizures, liver failure, and possibly death.

4. Alcohol & Yeast Dough
— Alcohol causes vomiting, incoordination, depression, tremors, coma. Yeast dough can bloat and twist the stomach and produce toxic alcohol internally.

5. Avocado (and its pit, skin, leaves)
— Persin may cause vomiting, diarrhea, heart issues, and pancreatitis; pits may cause choking or intestinal blockage.

6. Onions, Garlic, Chives, Leeks
— Damage red blood cells, causing anemia, vomiting, diarrhea, weakness.

7. Caffeine (coffee, tea, sodas, energy drinks)

— Can produce rapid heart rate, tremors, seizures, hyperactivity, possibly death.

8. Macadamia Nuts & Other Nuts (like almonds, walnuts)

— Macadamia nuts: weakness, tremors, hyperthermia, vomiting. Other nuts high in fat can lead to vomiting, diarrhea, pancreatitis.

9. Fruit Pits & Seeds (apricot, cherry, peach, plum, persimmon)

— Contain cyanide compounds; also present choking or blockage risk.

10. Raw or Cooked Bones

— Risk of splintering, choking, perforation of digestive tract, broken teeth.

11. Moldy Foods (aflatoxin)

— Can cause liver failure, tremors, seizures, vomiting, irregular heart rate, death.

12. Excessive Salt

— Can cause vomiting, diarrhea, dehydration, tremors, seizures.

13. Fatty or Fried Foods

— Lead to gastrointestinal upset, obesity, and pancreatitis.

14. Green Tomatoes & Potato "Green Parts"
— Solanine poisoning — vomiting, diarrhea, weakness.

15. Nutmeg
— Causes neurotoxicity — tremors, seizures, nervous system issues, potentially fatal.

16. Hops
— Can trigger malignant hyperthermia, often fatal.

17. Xylitol (in items beyond peanut butter: gum, toothpaste, candy)
— Same as peanut butter with xylitol: hypoglycemia, seizures, liver failure.

18. Household Human Medications and OTC Items (e.g., acetaminophen, ibuprofen, NSAIDs, decongestants, supplements)
— Many are highly toxic—e.g., acetaminophen is fatal to cats; NSAIDs cause GI ulceration, kidney damage; decongestants affect heart and blood pressure.

Signs to Watch For & What to Do If Noticed

Watch for:

• Vomiting or diarrhea

• Drooling or unusual salivation

• Lethargy or weakness

• Tremors, seizures, or incoordination

• Increased or decreased thirst and urination

• Abdominal pain or bloating

• Labored or rapid breathing

• Pale, yellowed, or bluish gums

• Collapse or unconsciousness

If you notice any of the above:

* Act immediately. Time is critical.
- Remove the pet from the source.
- Avoid giving any home remedies or inducing vomiting unless explicitly directed by a professional.
- Call a poison control hotline or your veterinarian right away.

- Provide essential info: pet's species, weight, what and how much was ingested, and when.
- Follow instructions carefully. Be prepared to go to an animal emergency clinic if advised.
- Monitor and record symptoms—this may be vital in ongoing assessment and treatment.

1.4 Emergency Contacts

Local Veterinarian:

____

Phone: ______________________

ASPCA Animal Poison Control Center (APCC)

Phone: **888-426-4435**

Available 24/7; consultation fee may apply

Pet Poison Helpline®

Phone: 855-764-7661

Available 24/7; incident fee applies

1.5 The Crunch Tweek

If you find yourself with a pup who likes that crunch, well then take a look here at some ways to make a crispier or crunchier biscuit that might get him rolling in the hay with happiness.
A few simple tweaks that'll turn those soft chews and puffs into firmer, crunchier biscuits that'll hold up longer in the feed sack (and give pups that satisfying crunch they love). Here are some cowboy-tested, kitchen-approved tricks you can work into your recipes:

1. Use less moisture
• Cut back slightly on wet ingredients (like yogurt, pumpkin, banana, etc.) so the dough's drier.
• The less wet the dough, the more it bakes into a crisp biscuit instead of a soft puff.

2. Add more oat flour
• oats soak up more liquid and bake into a firmer, sturdier treat.
• Rice flour also makes for a nice crunch, and it's gentle on tummies.

3. Bake longer at a lower temp
• After baking at 350°F, reduce the oven to 250°F and let the biscuits stay in another 20–30 minutes until they dry out.
• This turns them into a true "biscuit" instead of a soft cookie.

4. Thick oats or rolled cornmeal
• Thicker Rolled oats add texture and chewiness.

• Cornmeal bakes up grainy and firm, like a cowboy cornbread crust, but don't use if your pup has a corn allergy.

5. Flip them halfway through
• Flipping helps both sides dry evenly so they don't stay soft in the middle.

6. Cool in the oven
• After baking, turn the oven off and leave the treats inside while it cools down.
• This acts like a dehydrator and removes leftover moisture.,

1.6 Saddle Up and Ride On

Well, tarnation! Glad you didn't wander off yet, partner.

This here stretch of words is just meant to guide ya — it won't diagnose, it won't treat, not one lick of it's medical advice — just like that fine-print disclaimer you all saw up front. Me and that ornery pup Gruff, along with the Grub Wrangler, are downright tickled pink that you're fixing to try these biscuits. Don't reckon we're prouder — hope this old almanac's info helps ya wrangle success.

Now, you better remember, when it comes to your four-legged pals, always run it by a pro. My pups, my kittens — heck, they wouldn't be here if not for them. Expert folks were always just a phone call away, even when times were tougher than boot leather.

Vet bills don't come cheap — dogs cost an arm and a leg when you're patching them up. But I aim these biscuits to make their coats shine, their bones strong, and keep them riding around your porch for a long spell, maybe way off yonder at the far end of that Rainbow Bridge, but not anytime soon.

So quit lollygagging — saddle up and ride onward toward those puppy years.
Yee-haw!

Chapter 2 Puppy Days on the Range

Little Gruff chewed through a saddle strap once — thought it was jerky. That's when I knew I had to come up with something better for teething pups...

Health Watch:

From newborns to one year...

Common concerns:

- teething
- digestion
- growth rate
- early immune system development

Breed-specific notes

Top 10

1. Labrador Retriever

Watch out for = Keep an eye on food portions and weight gain since they easily become overweight. Choose food that supports joint health.

2. French Bulldog

Watch out for = Notice if they get gassy, itchy, or have loose stool — those are signs of food sensitivities. Choose digestible puppy food.

3. German Shepherd

Watch out for = Loose stool or tummy issues, plus rapid growth that stresses hips and elbows. Feed highly digestible, large-breed puppy food.

4. Golden Retriever

Watch out for = Extra weight and diets linked to heart issues. Stick with trusted large-breed puppy formulas, not grain-free unless vet-recommended.

5. Bulldog

Watch out for = Obesity, smelly gas, and skin flare-ups. Choose moderate-calorie, skin-friendly puppy food and avoid overfeeding.

6. Poodle

Watch out for = For toy poodles, prevent low blood sugar with multiple small meals. For standards, protect joints with balanced puppy food.

7. Beagle

Watch out for = They will beg for food constantly. Measure meals carefully and don't give high-fat table scraps.

8. Rottweiler

Watch out for = Growing too fast, which damages joints. Use large-breed puppy food, no calcium supplements, and keep them lean.

9. Dachshund

Watch out for = Extra weight strains their long back. Control portions and avoid calorie-dense treats.

10. German Shorthaired Pointer

Watch out for = Bloat risk (don't feed one giant meal). Feed several small meals, and support joints with large-breed puppy food.

General Puppy Nutrition Tips

All breeds

• Always feed puppy-specific food until skeletal maturity Varies: 12 months for small breeds, 18–24 months for large breeds.
• Avoid over-supplementing with calcium or vitamins unless prescribed.
• Maintain steady, lean growth — overweight puppies are much more likely to develop orthopedic disease.
• Make fresh water available, always.

Nutrition:

Focus on high-protein, DHA-rich, soft and chewy foods.

Ingredients To Help Puppies Grow:

- Goat milk
- Pumpkin
- Bone broth
- Eggs
- Oats
- Soft fruits

2.1 Pumpkin & Peanut Poppers

These little nuggets are a cowboy's best trick for keeping a pup's belly full and tail wagging. Easy to make, simple to store, and full of flavor dogs can't resist.

Ingredients:

- 1 cup canned pumpkin (plain, not pie filling)
- ½ cup natural peanut butter (xylitol-free — very important)
- 2 cups rolled oats (you can pulse them in a blender for a smoother texture if you like)
- 1 egg

Instructions:

1. Preheat your oven to 350°F (175°C). Line a baking sheet with parchment paper.
2. In a mixing bowl, stir together pumpkin, peanut butter, and egg until smooth.
3. Gradually add in the oats and mix until a soft dough forms.
4. Roll the dough into bite-sized balls or flatten and cut out small cookies
5. Place on the baking sheet and bake for 15–18 minutes, until firm to the touch.
6. Cool completely before serving.
7. Store in an airtight container in the fridge for up to a week, or freeze for longer storage.

Benefits:

• Pumpkin: Gentle on the tummy, full of fiber to help with digestion, and rich in vitamins A, C, and E.
• Peanut Butter: Packed with protein and healthy fats to keep a pup's energy steady on the trail.
• Oats: A wholesome grain that supports heart health and provides lasting fuel for playtime.
• Egg: A natural source of protein that helps support muscles, skin, and a shiny coat.

Gruff's Note:

Pumpkin, peanut butter, and oats? That's a trifecta of tail-wagging goodness. I'd trade my best stick for one of these — and that's saying something.

2.2 Cheddar Bites

For pups just finding their paws, these cheesy little nuggets are a gentle way to spoil 'them without upsetting their bellies. Soft enough for puppy teeth, tasty enough that older dogs will come trotting in too.

Ingredients:
- 1 cup finely shredded cheddar cheese (low-fat works best)
- 1-2/3 cup oat flour
- ¼ cup plain unsweetened yogurt
- 1 egg
- 2–3 tablespoons water (as needed to bring the dough together)

Instructions:

1. Preheat oven to 350°F (175°C). Line a baking sheet with parchment paper.
2. In a bowl, mix oat flour and cheese.
3. Add yogurt and egg, stirring until the dough starts to form.
4. If the dough feels too dry, add water a spoonful at a time until it holds together.
5. Roll into marble-sized balls or press and cut into flat bite-sized shapes.
6. Bake 12–15 minutes, until golden around the edges but still soft in the middle.
7. Let cool before serving.
8. Store in the fridge up to 5 days, or freeze for later.

Benefits:

- Cheddar Cheese: A source of calcium and protein, in small amounts it's a tasty training reward.
- Oat Flour: Fiber-rich and gentle on digestion.
- Yogurt: Provides probiotics that support a healthy gut.
- Egg: Builds strong muscles, a shiny coat, and healthy skin.

Gruff's Note:

Puppy or not, cheese makes the tail wag. Just watch out—if you leave the plate on the counter, I might just help myself. Purely in the name of quality control.

Chrissy Hartmann

2.3 Sweet Potato Nibbles

These soft, naturally sweet nibbles are perfect for pups learning the ropes—or for older dogs who just love a little taste of something special. Full of goodness and gentle on tiny tummies, they're a treat both you and your pup can feel good about.

Ingredients:

- 1 cup cooked and mashed sweet potato (plain, no spices)
- 1- 1/3 cups oat flour
- 1 egg
- 2 tablespoons natural peanut butter (xylitol-free)

Instructions:

1. Preheat your oven to 350°F (175°C) and line a baking sheet with parchment paper.
2. In a bowl, combine mashed sweet potato, egg, and peanut butter until smooth.
3. Gradually add the oat flour and mix until a soft dough forms.
4. Roll into small, bite-sized balls or press and cut into flat, tiny cookies.
5. Place on the baking sheet and bake 15–20 minutes, until firm but soft enough for puppy teeth.
6. Allow to cool completely before serving.
7. Store in an airtight container in the fridge for up to a week or freeze for later.

Benefits:

• Sweet Potato: Packed with fiber, vitamins A and C, and gentle on the digestive system.
• Peanut Butter: Provides protein and healthy fats for growing energy and tail-chasing stamina.
• Oat Flour: Supports heart and digestive health while adding a wholesome base.
• Egg: Strengthens muscles, coats, and skin.

Gruff's Note:

Sweet, soft, and mighty tasty! I promise to share...maybe. If you make these, keep a few extra handy—just in case I need a quality control sample or three.

Chrissy Hartmann

2.4 Banana Oat Bites

Soft, sweet, and full of natural energy, these bites are perfect for pups on the move—or just for those times when a little couch-side snack makes the day complete. Easy to make and gentle on tiny tummies, they're a treat worth wagging a tail over.

Ingredients:

- 1 ripe banana, mashed
- 1-1/3 cups rolled oats (pulse in a blender for finer texture if you like)
- 1 egg
- 2 tablespoons natural peanut butter (xylitol-free)

Instructions:

1. Preheat your oven to 350°F (175°C) and line a baking sheet with parchment paper.
2. In a bowl, mash the banana and stir in the egg and peanut butter until smooth.
3. Gradually add the oats and mix until a soft dough forms.
4. Roll the dough into small, bite-sized balls or flatten and cut into mini cookies.
5. Place on the baking sheet and bake 12–15 minutes, until firm but soft enough for puppy teeth.
6. Cool completely before serving.
7. Store in an airtight container in the fridge for up to a week, or freeze for later.

Benefits:

- Banana: Packed with potassium and natural energy, gentle on the tummy, and naturally sweet.
- Oats: Provide fiber and lasting fuel for playtime and tail-chasing adventures.
- Peanut Butter: Protein and healthy fats for growing muscles and happy tummies.
- Egg: Supports a shiny coat, strong muscles, and healthy skin.

Gruff's Note:

Banana and peanut butter? Now we're talking! These little bites are just the right size for sneaky snack missions. I might help myself while you're not looking, but I promise it's all in the name of quality control.

2.5 Chicken & Rice Mashies

Mild, tasty, and easy on tiny tummies, these little mashies are perfect for pups learning the ropes—or for grown dogs who just love a soft, wholesome bite. Packed with gentle protein and energy, they're a hit whether you're on the trail or lounging by the fire.

Ingredients:

- 1 cup cooked chicken, shredded (plain, no seasoning)
- ½ cup cooked brown rice
- 1 egg
- 2 tablespoons plain unsweetened yogurt
- ¼ cup oat flour

Instructions:

1. Preheat your oven to 350°F (175°C) and line a baking sheet with parchment paper.
2. In a bowl, mix shredded chicken, cooked rice, egg, and yogurt until combined.
3. Gradually stir in the flour until a soft dough forms.
4. Roll into small, bite-sized balls or flatten and cut into mini biscuits.
5. Place on the baking sheet and bake 15–18 minutes, until firm but soft enough for puppy teeth.
6. Cool completely before serving.
7. Store in an airtight container in the fridge for up to a week, or freeze for later.

Benefits:

• Chicken: Gentle protein to help build strong muscles.

• Rice: Easy-to-digest carbs that give pups energy without upsetting the tummy.

• Yogurt: A source of probiotics to support healthy digestion.

• Egg: Adds protein, supports healthy skin, and keeps coats shiny.

• Oat Flour: Provides fiber and wholesome texture without heaviness.

Gruff's Note:

Chicken and rice? Now we're talking real chow! Soft enough for tiny teeth, tasty enough that I'd do a happy dance for every bite. You might want to hide a few for later—trust me, I've got my eyes on them

.

2.6 Carrot Apple Chews

Crisp, naturally sweet, and packed with vitamins, these chews are perfect for little pups with a growing appetite — or older dogs who just enjoy a crunchy, wholesome treat. Easy to make, tasty to munch, and gentle on tummies, they're a real tail-wagger.

Ingredients:

- 1 cup finely grated carrot
- 1 cup finely grated apple (peeled, seeds removed)
- 1 cup oat flour
- 1 egg
- 1 tablespoon natural peanut butter xylitol-free

Instructions:

1. Preheat your oven to 350°F (175°C) and line a baking sheet with parchment paper.
2. In a bowl, mix grated carrot, apple, egg, and peanut butter until well combined.
3. Gradually stir in the flour until a soft, slightly sticky dough forms.
4. Roll into small, bite-sized balls or flatten and cut into mini chews.
5. Place on the baking sheet and bake 12–15 minutes, until lightly golden but still soft enough for puppy teeth.
6. Cool completely before serving.
7. Store in an airtight container in the fridge for up to a week, or freeze for longer storage.

Benefits:

• Carrot: Crunchy, full of beta-carotene, and supports healthy teeth and vision.
• Apple: Naturally sweet, provides fiber, and is packed with vitamins.
• Peanut Butter: Adds protein and healthy fats for energy and happy tails.
• Egg: Supports muscles, skin, and coat health.
• Oat Flour: Gentle on digestion, fiber-rich, and a wholesome base.

Gruff's Note:

Carrot, apple, and peanut butter? Don't let the fancy name fool you—these chews are mighty tasty! I'll happily volunteer as the chief taste tester. Might need to sneak a few while you're not looking.

2.7 Goat Milk Biscuits

Rich, creamy, and gentle on tiny tummies, these biscuits are perfect for pups who need a little extra nourishment or just love a soft, wholesome treat. Easy to make and full of goodness, they're a tail-wagging favorite on the trail—or at home by the fire.

Ingredients:

- 1-1/3 cups oat flour
- ¼ cup goat milk
- 1 egg
- 2 tablespoons natural peanut butter, xylitol-free
- 1 teaspoon pumpkin puree (optional, for extra flavor and fiber)

Instructions:

1. Preheat your oven to 350°F (175°C) and line a baking sheet with parchment paper.
2. In a bowl, mix oat flour, egg, peanut butter, and pumpkin puree (if using) until combined.
3. Gradually add goat milk until a soft dough forms.
4. Roll into small, bite-sized balls or flatten and cut into mini biscuits.
5. Place on the baking sheet and bake 12–15 minutes, until lightly golden and firm enough to hold shape.
6. Allow to cool completely before serving.
7. Store in an airtight container in the fridge for up to a week, or freeze for later.

Benefits:

- Goat Milk: Gentle on digestion, rich in nutrients, and easy for puppies to absorb.
- Peanut Butter: Protein and healthy fats for growing energy and happy tails.
- Pumpkin: Fiber-rich, supports healthy digestion, and adds a touch of natural sweetness.
- Egg: Supports strong muscles, skin, and a shiny coat.
- Oat Flour: Provides fiber and a wholesome base, gentle on puppy tummies.

Gruff's Note:

Goat milk? Fancy, huh? Let me tell ya, it's smooth, tasty, and worth every lick. I'll be your chief taste tester—might even polish off a few before you get a chance to see them.

2.8 Blueberry Blue Bones

Juicy, sweet, and packed with antioxidants, these little bites are perfect for pups who love a fruity surprise—or for older dogs who just enjoy a wholesome, tasty treat. Soft, chewy, and tail-waggingly good, they're easy to make and gentle on tiny tummies.

Ingredients:

- 1 cup fresh or frozen blueberries (thawed if frozen)
- 1-3/4 cup oat flour
- 1 egg
- 2 tablespoons natural peanut butter (xylitol-free)
- 1 tablespoon plain yogurt (optional, for added creaminess)

Instructions:

1. Preheat your oven to 350°F (175°C) and line a baking sheet with parchment paper.
2. In a bowl, mash the blueberries slightly and stir in the egg, peanut butter, and yogurt (if using) until smooth.
3. Gradually fold in the oat flour until a soft dough forms.
4. Roll into small, bite-sized balls or flatten and cut out mini cookies.
5. Place on the baking sheet and bake 12–15 minutes, until lightly firm but still soft for puppy teeth.
6. Cool completely before serving.
7. Store in an airtight container in the fridge for up to a week, or freeze for later.

Benefits:

• Blueberries: Rich in antioxidants, vitamins, and fiber for a healthy, happy pup.
• Peanut Butter: Protein and healthy fats to keep tails wagging and energy steady.
• Yogurt: Optional probiotics to support good digestion.
• Egg: Builds strong muscles, healthy skin, and shiny coats.
• Oat Flour: Gentle on tummies and adds a wholesome, hearty texture.

Gruff's Note:

Blueberries, eh? Tiny bursts of yum in every bite! I'll happily volunteer as the official taste tester...might even need to do a few rounds to make sure they pass the 'paw of approval.' Safety first, treats second.

Chrissy Hartmann

2.9 Salmon Softies

Rich, savory, and loaded with healthy goodness, these chews are perfect for pups who fancy a taste of the sea. Soft enough for puppy teeth yet hearty enough for older dogs, they're packed with protein and omega-3s to keep tails wagging strong.

Ingredients:

- 1 cup cooked salmon, flaked (plain, no seasoning or skin)
- 1-2/3 cup oat flour
- 1 egg
- 2 tablespoons plain unsweetened yogurt
- 1 tablespoon olive oil (optional, for extra healthy fats)
- 1 tablespoon water if dough is dry

Instructions:

1. Preheat your oven to 350°F (175°C) and line a baking sheet with parchment paper.
2. In a bowl, combine salmon, egg, yogurt, and olive oil until mixed.
3. Stir in the flour gradually until a dough forms.
4. Roll into bite-sized balls or flatten and cut out mini biscuits.
5. Place on the baking sheet and bake 15–18 minutes, until lightly golden and firm to the touch.
6. Cool completely before serving.
7. Store in an airtight container in the fridge up to 5 days, or freeze for longer.

Benefits:

• Salmon: Rich in omega-3 fatty acids to support brain development, shiny coats, and healthy joints.
• Yogurt: Provides probiotics for good digestion and gut health.
• Egg: Protein to build strong muscles and keep pups growing strong.
• Oat Flour: A gentle, wholesome base that's easy to digest.
• Olive Oil: Optional healthy fats to keep coats glossy and skin smooth.

Gruff's Note:

Salmon, you say? Count me in! These chews smell so good I might start circling the kitchen like a hungry coyote. Don't be surprised if I 'accidentally' taste-test a whole batch...better safe than sorry, right?

2.10 Mini Liver Puffs

Rich, savory, and downright irresistible, these puffs are the kind of treat pups will follow their nose clear across the ranch to find. Light and fluffy on the outside, full of protein on the inside, they're perfect for training rewards or just spoiling a pup who's been extra good.

Ingredients:

- ½ cup cooked beef or chicken liver, finely- chopped or pureed
- 1-1/2 cups oat flour
- 1 egg
- 2 tablespoons plain unsweetened yogurt
- 1 tablespoon olive oil or coconut oil

Instructions:

1. Preheat oven to 350°F (175°C) and line a baking sheet with parchment paper.
2. In a bowl, mix liver, egg, yogurt, and oil until blended.
3. Stir in the flour until a thick batter forms.
4. Drop small spoonfuls onto the baking sheet — think bite-sized "puffs."
5. Bake 12–15 minutes, until puffed up and lightly golden.
6. Cool completely before serving.
7. Store in the fridge up to 4–5 days, or freeze for later.

Benefits:

- Liver: Packed with iron, vitamins A and B, and protein for strong muscles and energy.
- Yogurt: Adds probiotics to support digestion.
- Egg: Builds healthy skin, shiny coats, and sturdy growth.
- Oat Flour: Gentle, fiber-rich base that's easy on puppy tummies.
- Olive or Coconut Oil: Healthy fats that keep skin smooth and coats glossy.

Gruff's Note:

Mini puffs, big flavor! You put these on the counter, and I'll be sitting pretty faster than you can say 'good dog.' Just don't blink—or the whole batch might vanish quicker than a jackrabbit on the prairie.

The Grub Wrangler's Wisdom:

Don't go fancy — go functional.

These biscuits are made to build bodies and train minds. Keep 'em soft, and watch those little teeth. And the senior pups who like a little softer chew after all the years of wrangling leather and rope will love them too.

The Cowpoke's Baking Notes:

Chrissy Hartmann

Chapter 3 Prime Time Trailblazers

Gruff used to chase coyotes—and come back for his biscuit like it was payday. He needed fuel to stay fast and strong.

Health Watch:

For 1 to 7 year olds

Common concerns:

- Joint health
- Weight management
- Energy
- Allergies

Breed considerations:
1. Labrador Retriever

Prime-age risks:
• Obesity leading to joint problems and diabetes.
• Hip and elbow dysplasia.
• Cruciate ligament tears (knee injuries).

2. French Bulldog

Prime-age risks:
• Breathing difficulties (brachycephalic airway syndrome).
• Skin fold infections.
• Spinal disorders (hemivertebrae, IVDD).

3. German Shepherd

Prime-age risks:
• Hip and elbow dysplasia.
• Degenerative myelopathy (nerve/spinal condition, later onset but can start showing signs).
• Chronic digestive issues (sensitive gut, IBD).

4. Golden Retriever

Prime-age risks:
• Cancer (lymphoma, hemangiosarcoma — unfortunately high rates in Goldens).
• Hip/elbow dysplasia.
• Skin allergies and ear infections.

5. Bulldog (English Bulldog)

Prime-age risks:
• Breathing problems from narrow airways.
• Overheating/heatstroke.
• Skin fold infections.
• Early-onset arthritis due to abnormal joint structure.

6. Poodle (Standard / Miniature / Toy)

Prime-age risks:
• Standards: hip dysplasia, bloat (gastric dilatation-volvulus).
• Minis/Toys: luxating patella (kneecap slips), dental disease.
• All: Addison's disease (hormonal).

7. Beagle

Prime-age risks:
• Obesity leading to diabetes and arthritis.
• Epilepsy (seizures are relatively common).
• Hypothyroidism (low thyroid function).

8. Rottweiler

Prime-age risks:
• Hip and elbow dysplasia.
• Cruciate ligament tears.
• Cancer (osteosarcoma = bone cancer is common in Rotties).

9. Dachshund

Prime-age risks:
• Intervertebral disc disease (back problems, paralysis risk).
• Obesity worsening spinal issues.
• Dental disease (especially minis).

10. German Shorthaired Pointer

Prime-age risks:
• Bloat/GDV (life-threatening if stomach twists).
• Hip dysplasia.
• Epilepsy and some autoimmune conditions.

The Big Picture

Breeds (Labs, Goldens, Shepherds, Rotties, Pointers, Standard Poodles): Joint issues, bloat, cancers.

Small/medium breeds (Frenchie, Beagle, Dachshund, Toy Poodle): Obesity, spinal issues, dental disease, allergies.

Flat-faced breeds (Frenchie, Bulldog): Breathing and skin issues.

Nutrition:

• **Balanced macros:** Lean protein, fiber, glucosamine-rich foods.
• **Add anti-inflammatory foods:** Turmeric and ginger.

Chrissy Hartmann

3.1 Turmeric Chicken Crunchies

Here's a treat built tough, just like the working dogs out on the range. These crunchy biscuits pack the goodness of chicken and the golden spice turmeric, known for keeping joints limber and bellies calm. Perfect for those middle years when pups still run like the wind but can use a little extra help staying spry.

Ingredients:

- 1 cup cooked chicken, finely chopped or shredded
- 1-½ cup rolled oats
- 1 egg
- ½ cup chicken broth (no or low sodium)
- ½ teaspoon ground turmeric
- 1 tablespoon olive oil

Instructions:

1. Preheat oven to 350°F (175°C) and line a baking sheet with parchment paper.
2. Mix chicken, egg, broth, oil, and turmeric in a bowl.
3. Stir in oat flour until a dough forms. If sticky, add a bit more flour.
4. Roll out dough ¼-inch thick and cut into shapes with a cookie cutter or knife.
5. Bake 25–30 minutes until golden and firm.
6. Store in an airtight container up to a week, or freeze for later.

Benefits:

- Chicken: Lean protein that fuels energy and strong muscles.
- Turmeric: Natural anti-inflammatory to support joint health and reduce stiffness.
- Oat Flour: Gentle on digestion, rich in fiber.
- Olive Oil: Healthy fats that keep coats shiny and soft.

Gruff's Note:

Golden biscuits, huh? Suits me just fine! If these help keep my joints moving, I'll chase that tumbleweed all day long. Just don't expect me to share with the neighbor's cat.

3.2 Apple & Flax Discs

A little sweet, a little hearty—these biscuits bring the best of the orchard to the chuckwagon. Crisp apple meets nutty flaxseed in a crunchy disc built to keep bellies happy and coats shining. Perfect for dogs who still chase after every squirrel, but need steady fuel to keep them going.

Ingredients:

- 1 medium apple, peeled, cored, and finely grated
- 1-1/3 cups oat flour
- ½ cup ground flaxseed
- 1 egg
- 2 tablespoons plain unsweetened yogurt
- 2 tablespoons olive oil
- ¼ cup water (as needed)

Instructions:

1. Preheat oven to 350°F (175°C) and line a baking sheet with parchment paper.
2. Combine grated apple, egg, yogurt, and oil in a bowl.
3. Stir in flaxseed and oats until dough forms. Add water a little at a time if needed.
4. Roll dough ¼-inch thick and cut into round discs (a jar lid works just fine if you don't have cutters handy).
5. Bake 25–30 minutes until firm and lightly golden.
6. Store in an airtight container up to a week, or freeze for later adventures.

Benefits:

- Apple: Adds natural sweetness, fiber, and vitamin C for immune support.
- Flaxseed: Loaded with omega-3s for shiny coats and anti-inflammatory support.
- Yogurt: Provides probiotics to aid digestion.
- Oats: Gentle fiber to keep the digestive system running smooth.

Gruff's Note:

Discs, huh? Sounds fancy. But to me, they're just tasty round treasures — and I'll happily sniff out a whole batch if you let me. Don't worry, I'll leave you a crumb or two… maybe.

3.3 Parsley Mint Biscuits

For all the love dogs give, their breath doesn't always return the favor. These crunchy biscuits bring together fresh mint and parsley to keep kisses sweet and tummies calm. Perfect for trail dogs and couch companions alike, they're a breath-saver and a tail-wagger rolled into one.

Ingredients:

- 1-1/3 cups oat flour
- ½ cup rolled oats
- 1 egg
- ¼ cup fresh parsley, finely chopped
- 2 tablespoons fresh mint leaves, finely chopped
- 2 tablespoons coconut oil
- ½ cup water (as needed)

Instructions:

1. Preheat oven to 325°F (160°C) and line a baking sheet with parchment paper.
2. In a bowl, whisk egg and coconut oil together.
3. Stir in parsley, mint, oats, and flour. Add water slowly until a firm dough forms.
4. Roll dough ¼-inch thick and cut into shapes (bones, hearts, or whatever suits your pup).
5. Bake 25–30 minutes until dry and crunchy.
6. Store in an airtight container for up to a week, or freeze for longer storage.

Benefits:

- Mint & Parsley: Freshen breath naturally while supporting digestion.
- Coconut Oil: Adds healthy fats for shiny coats and healthy skin.
- Oats: Gentle fiber that keeps the digestive system steady.
- Egg: Builds strong muscles and adds a little protein punch.

Gruff's Note:

Minty fresh? That means more smooches, right? I'll wag my tail, lean in close, and make sure you know these biscuits worked. Fair trade if you ask me!

3.4 Cheddar & Oat Chompers

Sharp, savory, and downright satisfying –
these crunchy biscuits bring the goodness of cheddar cheese together with hearty oats. Built for dogs who still have plenty of pep in their step, they're the kind of trail snack that makes sitting, staying, and rolling over worth every wag.

Ingredients:

- 1 cup shredded sharp cheddar cheese
- 1 1/3 cups oat flour
- ½ cup rolled oats
- 1 egg
- 2 tablespoons olive oil
- ¼ cup low salt beef broth
- ¼ cup water (as needed)

Instructions:

1. Preheat oven to 350°F (175°C) and line a baking sheet with parchment paper.
2. Mix cheese, egg, beef broth, and oil in a bowl until blended.
3. Stir in rolled oats and flour, adding water a little at a time until dough comes together.
4. Roll dough ¼-inch thick and cut into bone or square shapes.
5. Bake 20–25 minutes until golden and firm.
6. Store in an airtight container up to a week, or freeze for later.

Benefits:

• Cheddar Cheese: A tasty source of calcium and protein (in moderation).
• Oats & Oat Flour: Provide gentle fiber for steady digestion.
• Egg: Builds strong muscles and keeps energy levels steady.
• Olive Oil: Healthy fats that help with shiny coats and smooth skin.
• Beef Broth: Tasty source of protein.

Gruff's Note:

Cheese? Say no more—I'm sold! You pull these out, and I'll be lined up straighter than a rodeo horse at the gate. Don't mind the drool, partner — it's part of the show.

3.5 Salmon & Chia Coins

These little coins shine brighter than a silver buckle at the county fair. Packed with omega-rich salmon and crunchy chia seeds, they're built to keep coats glossy, joints flexible, and tails wagging high. A smart choice for those middle years when pups still run hard but could use a little extra shine and support.

Ingredients:

- 1 cup cooked salmon, flaked (no bones, no skin)
- 1 ½ cups oat flour
- 2 tablespoons chia seeds
- ½ cup rolled oats
- 1 egg
- 1 tablespoon olive oil
- ¼ cup water (as needed)

Instructions:

1. Preheat oven to 350°F (175°C) and line a baking sheet with parchment paper.
2. Mix salmon, egg, oil, and water in a bowl until blended.
3. Stir in flour, chia seeds, and oats until a firm dough forms.
4. Roll out dough ¼-inch thick and cut into small round "coins" with a cutter or jar lid.
5. Bake 20–25 minutes until golden and crisp.
6. Store in the fridge for up to a week, or freeze for later use.

Benefits:

• Salmon: Rich in omega-3 fatty acids for joint health and shiny coats.
• Chia Seeds: Packed with fiber, protein, and healthy fats to support digestion and energy.
• Oats & Oat Flour: Gentle on stomachs while keeping digestion steady.
• Egg: Adds protein and nutrients for strong muscles.

Gruff's Note:

Coins, huh? Well, partner, I'll take these over gold any day. You flip me one of these beauties, and I'll fetch it faster than a prospector chasing pay dirt.

3.6 Joint Support Jerky Bites

These bites are built tough and made to last—kind of like the old ranch hounds that never quit. Packed with lean protein, boosted with turmeric and flax, and finished with just the right chew, they're tailor-made for keeping joints limber and tails high. Perfect for long hikes, ranch rounds, or just keeping a dog spry enough to jump in the truck bed without a second thought.

Ingredients:

- 1 lb ground turkey or chicken
- ½ cup oat flour
- 2 tablespoons ground flaxseed
- 1 teaspoon ground turmeric
- 1 egg
- 1 tablespoon olive oil

Instructions:

1. Preheat oven to 325°F (160°C) and line a baking sheet with parchment paper.
2. Mix all ingredients in a bowl until well combined.
3. Spread mixture onto the sheet about ¼-inch thick.
4. Score into small bite-sized squares with a knife.
5. Bake 25–30 minutes until firm, then flip and bake another 15–20 minutes to dry out.
6. Cool completely before breaking into jerky-style bites.
7. Store in the fridge up to a week, or freeze for later.

Benefits:

- Ground Turkey/Chicken: Lean protein to fuel energy without extra fat.
- Flaxseed: Omega-3 fatty acids for joint comfort and coat health.
- Turmeric: Natural anti-inflammatory to ease stiffness.
- Olive Oil: Healthy fats that support skin and joint flexibility.

Gruff's Note:

Jerky? Now you're talking my language! These bites keep me moving smoother than a calf roper on Sunday morning. Toss a few my way, and I'll show you I've still got plenty of kick left in me.

Chrissy Hartmann

3.7 Beef & Sweet Tater Rounds

Nothing says trail fuel like beef and taters. These crunchy biscuits mix lean ground beef with the natural sweetness of sweet potatoes for a treat that keeps pups full of zip while supporting steady digestion. Built for the middle years, they've got just the right balance of protein and fiber to keep your dog charging fences, chasing rabbits, or napping like a champ after chores are done.

Ingredients:

- 1 cup cooked lean ground beef, crumbled and cooled
- 1 cup mashed sweet potato (plain, no butter or sugar)
- 1 1/3 cups oat flour
- ½ cup rolled oats
- 1 egg
- 1 tablespoon olive oil

Instructions:

1. Preheat oven to 350°F (175°C) and line a baking sheet with parchment paper.
2. In a bowl, mix beef, mashed sweet potato, egg, and oil.
3. Stir in flour and oats until a firm dough forms.
4. Roll dough ¼-inch thick and cut into bone or round shapes.
5. Bake 25–30 minutes until golden and crisp.
6. Store in an airtight container up to a week, or freeze for later.

Benefit:

- Beef: Protein-rich fuel for muscle strength and energy.
- Sweet Potato: Fiber and beta-carotene to aid digestion and support eye health.
- Oats & Oat Flour: Gentle fiber that keeps bellies balanced.
- Olive Oil: Healthy fats for shiny coats and supple joints.

Gruff's Note:

Beef and taters? Now that's a cowboy supper I can get behind. Serve me these biscuits, and I'll guard the chuckwagon like it's Fort Knox.

3.8 Kale & Peanut Butter Pucks

Don't let the greens fool you—these pucks are pure pup-pleasing goodness. Kale brings the vitamins, peanut butter brings the flavor, and together they bake up into crunchy snacks that'll have dogs begging for more. A smart choice for keeping pups fueled, shiny, and spry through their middle years.

Ingredients:

- 1 cup fresh kale, finely chopped (stems removed)
- ½ cup natural peanut butter (xylitol-free, unsalted)
- 1 1/3 cups oat flour
- ½ cup rolled oats
- 1 egg
- ¼ cup water (as needed)

Instructions:

1. Preheat oven to 350°F (175°C) and line a baking sheet with parchment paper.
2. In a bowl, mix peanut butter, egg, and water until smooth.
3. Stir in chopped kale, oats, and flour until a firm dough forms.
4. Roll into balls, flatten slightly into "pucks," and place on the baking sheet.
5. Bake 25–30 minutes until golden and crisp. 6. Store in an airtight container up to a week, or freeze for later trail snacks.

Benefits:
• Kale: Packed with vitamins A, C, and K for immune support and strong bones.
• Peanut Butter: Protein and healthy fats for energy and shiny coats.
• Oats & Oat Flour: Gentle fiber for balanced digestion.
• Egg: Adds protein and helps hold everything together.

Gruff's Note:
Greens and peanut butter? Now that's a trick worthy of a cowboy cook! I don't even notice the kale—I'm too busy licking the peanut butter off my chops. Toss me another puck, and I'll fetch it quicker than a lasso on a runaway calf.

3.9 Pumpkin Seed Crisps

Light, crisp, and full of earthy flavor, these biscuits pack the mighty pumpkin seed into every bite. Known for boosting muscle health and adding a little shine to a dog's coat, these crisps are a smart, crunchy choice for pups in their prime. Serve them up on the porch, in the pasture, or straight from the chuckwagon tin.

Ingredients:

- ½ cup raw, unsalted pumpkin seeds (ground or finely chopped)
- 1 1/3 cups oat flour
- ½ cup rolled oats
- ½ cup pumpkin puree (plain, not spiced)
- 1 egg
- 2 tablespoons olive oil
- ¼ cup water (as needed)

Instructions:

1. Preheat oven to 350°F (175°C) and line a baking sheet with parchment paper.
2. In a bowl, mix pumpkin puree, egg, and oil until smooth.
3. Stir in pumpkin seeds, flour, and oats. Add water slowly until a firm dough forms.
4. Roll dough ¼-inch thick and cut into squares or discs.
5. Bake 25–30 minutes until golden and crisp.
6. Store in an airtight container up to a week, or freeze for longer storage.

Benefits:

• Pumpkin Seeds: Rich in protein, iron, and healthy fats to support strong muscles and shiny coats.
• Pumpkin Puree: Gentle fiber to aid digestion and keep bellies balanced.
• Oats & Oat Flour: Provide steady energy and keep things easy on the gut.
• Olive Oil: Helps joints stay flexible and coats stay glossy.

Gruff's Note:

Seeds in a crisp? I'll take a pawful, thanks kindly! These little beauties crunch loud enough to turn heads clear across the barnyard. Don't blame me if I come sniffing around for seconds.

3.10 Quinoa Carrot Crunch

Tiny grains, big flavor, and just the right crunch—these biscuits mix protein-packed quinoa with sweet carrots to keep pups energized, spry, and chomping happily. Perfect for dogs in their middle years who still love to roam the pasture, chase a stick, or keep an eye on the chuckwagon.

Ingredients:

- ½ cup cooked quinoa, cooled
-1 medium carrot, grated
- 1-2/3 cups oat flour
- 1 egg
- 2 tablespoons olive oil
- 2–3 tablespoons water, as needed

Instructions:

1. Preheat oven to 350°F (175°C) and line a baking sheet with parchment paper.
2. In a bowl, mix grated carrot, quinoa, egg, and olive oil until combined.
3. Stir in flour until a firm dough forms. Add water a little at a time if needed.
4. Roll dough ¼-inch thick and cut into sticks, squares, or fun shapes.
5. Bake 25–30 minutes until lightly golden and crunchy.
6. Store in an airtight container up to a week, or freeze for later.

Benefits:

• Quinoa: Complete protein with all essential amino acids to support lean muscle.
• Carrot: Fiber, beta-carotene, and natural sweetness for healthy digestion and bright eyes.
• Oat Flour: Gentle fiber for steady energy and easy digestion.
• Olive Oil: Healthy fats that keep joints flexible and coats shiny.

Gruff's Note:

Quinoa, carrots, and crunch? Sounds fancy, but I'll tell ya what—it's delicious! I'll happily taste-test each one, just to make sure you didn't skimp. Quality control is serious business, partner!

The Grub Wrangler's Wisdom:

Middle age ain't the end of the trail — it's just time to ride smarter. These treats keep the fire burning without clogging up the furnace.

The Cowpokes Baking Notes:

Chrissy Hartmann

Chapter 4 Senior Sidekicks

Old Gruff walks slower, but his tail still wags like a flag in a storm. His favorite now is a biscuit I call 'Golden Delights.'

Health Watch:

For 8+ year old dogs

Concerns:

- Arthritis
- dental decline
- organ support
- cognition.

Breed-specific risks:

Senior Dogs

Large dogs 7 years old and small dogs 10 years old

1. Labrador Retriever (senior at ~7+)

- Arthritis and mobility issues (hips, elbows, knees).
- Obesity-related conditions (diabetes, heart disease).
- Cancer (especially mast cell tumors and lymphoma).
- Hearing and vision loss.

2. French Bulldog (senior at ~9–10+)

- Worsening breathing problems (brachycephalic airway disease).
- Spinal disease (IVDD).
- Chronic skin infections.
- Heart disease (pulmonic stenosis, cardiomyopathy).

3. German Shepherd (senior at ~7+)

- Degenerative myelopathy (progressive paralysis of hind legs).
- Severe arthritis and hip/elbow dysplasia progression.
- Chronic GI issues.
- Increased cancer risk (hemangiosarcoma, lymphoma).

4. Golden Retriever (senior at ~7+)

- High cancer risk (hemangiosarcoma, lymphoma).
- Arthritis and mobility problems.
- Hypothyroidism.
- Cataracts and other eye issues.

5. Bulldog (English Bulldog, senior at ~8–9+)

- Severe arthritis from abnormal joints.
- Chronic respiratory problems (worsen with age).
- Heart disease.
- Increased risk of overheating, even at rest.

6. Poodle

• Standard (senior at ~7–8+): Bloat, arthritis, cancer (especially hemangiosarcoma).
• Mini/Toy (senior at ~10–11+): Dental disease, heart murmurs/mitral valve disease, tracheal collapse.
• All sizes: Cushing's or Addison's disease (hormonal).

7. Beagle (senior at ~9–10+)

• Obesity leading to arthritis and diabetes.
• Hypothyroidism.
• Cancer (mammary tumors, lymphoma).
• Hearing loss (common in older Beagles).

8. Rottweiler (senior at ~7+)

• Osteosarcoma (bone cancer, very common in seniors).
• Arthritis and hip/elbow dysplasia progression.
• Heart problems (aortic stenosis, cardiomyopathy).
• Obesity-related health issues.

9. Dachshund (senior at ~10–11+)

• Severe back disease (IVDD, paralysis risk increases).
• Arthritis, especially in long spines and short legs.
• Obesity worsening spinal/joint issues.
• Dental disease.

10. German Shorthaired Pointer (senior at ~7–8+)

- Bloat/GDV risk remains lifelong.
- Arthritis and hip dysplasia.
- Cancer (mast cell tumors, lymphoma).
- Laryngeal paralysis (airway problems in older, large breeds).

Key Senior Dog Themes:

Large breeds (Lab, Shepherd, Golden, Rottie, GSP, Standard Poodle) → arthritis, cancer, bloat, heart problems.

Small/medium breeds (Frenchie, Bulldog, Beagle, Dachshund, Toy/Minis) → obesity, dental disease, breathing problems, spinal issues.

All breeds slower metabolism, decreased mobility, higher risk of chronic disease.

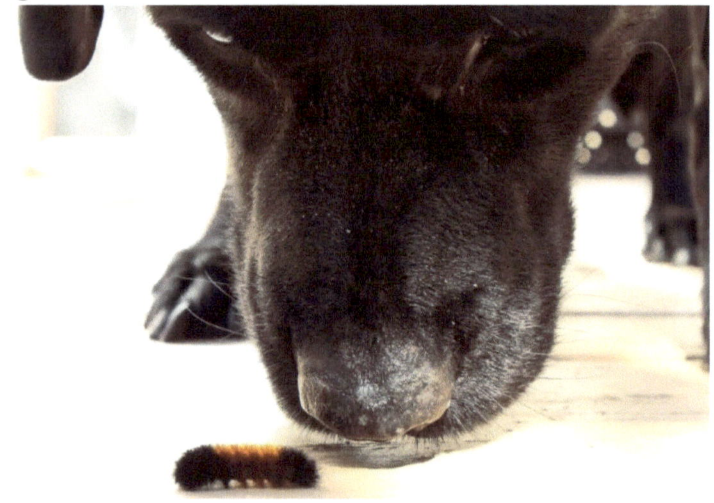

Nutrition:

• Focus on digestibility, antioxidants, low-fat, joint and brain support.

• Add bone broth, turmeric, blueberries, and coconut oil.

Now follow this here trail for 10 senior dog biscuits ...

Chrissy Hartmann

4.1 Pumpkin Turmeric Biscuits

Now listen here—senior dogs got tender bellies and stiff joints, same as an old trail hand after too many nights sleeping on a bedroll. This here recipe ain't fancy, but it'll do the trick. Pumpkin keeps their guts running smooth, and turmeric's good for the creaks in their bones. Don't argue with me — it's doggone science.

Ingredients:

- 1 cup canned pumpkin, plain, not pie filling
- 2 1/3 cups oat flour
- 1 egg
- 2 tablespoons ground flaxseed
- 1 teaspoon ground turmeric
- ¼ teaspoon black pepper, helps turmeric work better
- 2 tablespoons olive oil
- ¼ cup water (add more if dough's too dry)

Instructions:

1. Preheat the oven to 350°F, 175°C, and line a baking sheet with parchment paper.
2. In a big bowl, stir together pumpkin, egg, flaxseed, turmeric, pepper, and olive oil until smooth.
3. Add flour a little at a time, mixing until dough holds together. Splash in water if it gets too crumbly.
4. Roll out dough on a floured surface to ¼ inch thick.
5. Cut into bone shapes (or squares if you don't fuss with cutters).
6. Place biscuits on the baking sheet and bake 25–30 minutes until firm and golden.
7. Let cool completely before serving — unless you like burnt paws and singed whiskers.

Benefits:

- Pumpkin: High in fiber for digestion and gentle on sensitive stomachs.
- Turmeric + black pepper: Natural anti-inflammatory to help ease stiff joints and arthritis.
- Flaxseed: Packed with omega-3s for skin, coat, and heart health.
- Olive oil: Keeps joints lubricated and fur shiny.

Gruff's Note:

Well, ain't this a fine surprise — cookies that don't taste like cardboard. Pumpkin makes it sweet, turmeric keeps my creaky hips from squeaking like a rusty gate, and flaxseed? Don't let them fool ya — it ain't bird food, it's dog fuel. Just don't go eating them yourself, unless you're partial to biscuits with a kick.

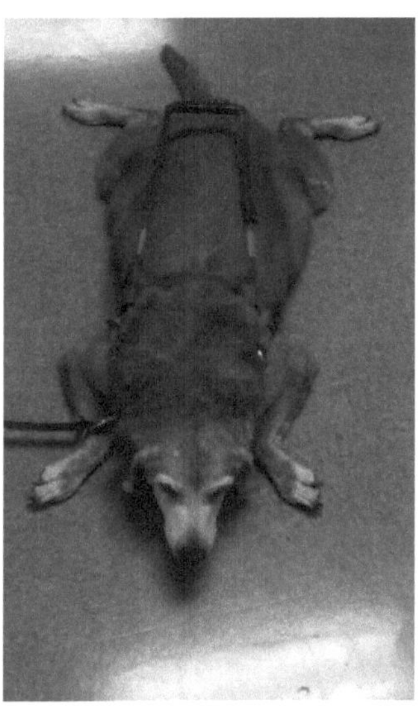

4.2 Blueberry Soft Chews

Old dogs deserve a little sweetness without wrecking their teeth. These soft chews go down easy, and blueberries pack a wallop of goodness. Do not start jawing about sugar — blueberries are the kind of sweet a body can respect. Keeps their brains sharp, their bellies happy, and their tails thumping

Ingredients:

- 1 cup fresh or frozen blueberries (no syrup, no sugar added)
- 1 ripe banana, mashed
- 1 egg
- 1 tablespoon honey (optional, if your vet approves)
- 2 cups oat flour (or grind rolled oats fine in a blender)
- ½ cup unsweetened applesauce
- 1 tablespoon coconut oil

Instructions:

1. Preheat oven to 325°F, 160°C, and line a baking sheet with parchment paper.
2. Mash banana in a mixing bowl until smooth, then stir in applesauce, coconut oil, egg, and honey.
3. Fold in blueberries gently so you do not mash them all to bits.
4. Add oat flour a little at a time until dough holds together but stays soft.
5. Drop spoonfuls onto baking sheet and press lightly with the back of the spoon.
6. Bake 18–20 minutes until set but still tender.
7. Cool before serving so your dog does not scorch his tongue.

Benefits:

• Blueberries: Rich in antioxidants that support brain health and fight aging.
• Banana: Gentle source of potassium for muscle function.
• Oats: Easy to digest, high in fiber for gut health.
• Coconut oil: Supports coat shine and may aid cognitive function.

Gruff's Note:

Finally, a treat soft enough that I do not have to wrestle it with my molars like a rawhide. Blueberries keep me thinking sharp, so I can remember exactly where I buried your favorite boot. Banana makes it sweet without turning it into candy. Go on, hand me two — you owe me for the time I did not chase the mailman... much.

4.3 Bone Broth Biscuits

Dogs getting up there in years need more than belly rubs and soft beds. They need strength in their bones and oil in their joints. That is where these biscuits come in. Bone broth makes the base hearty, and turmeric gives it a kick against the aches. Do not go wasting time on fancy garnishes — this is honest food for hard-working dogs.

Ingredients:

- 1 cup bone broth (unsalted, no onion or garlic)
- 2 1/3 cups oat flour
- 1 egg
- 1 tablespoon olive oil
- 1 teaspoon ground turmeric
- ¼ teaspoon black pepper
- 2 tablespoons powdered milk, optional, for extra calcium

Instructions:

1. Preheat oven to 350°F, 175°C, and line a baking sheet with parchment paper.
2. In a mixing bowl, whisk together bone broth, egg, olive oil, turmeric, and pepper.
3. Stir in flour gradually until dough forms. If too sticky, add more flour; if too dry, splash in a little more broth.
4. Roll dough out to about ¼ inch thick.
5. Cut into bone shapes or squares and place on the baking sheet.
6. Bake 25–30 minutes until firm and golden around the edges.
7. Let cool completely before letting your old hound sink his teeth in.

Benefits:

• Bone broth: Rich in collagen and minerals that support joint and bone health.
• Turmeric + black pepper: Natural anti-inflammatory combo for stiff joints.
• Olive oil: Keeps coats shiny and joints lubricated.
• Powdered milk: Extra calcium for strong bones and teeth.

Gruff's Note:

Now this is my kind of biscuit — savory, hearty, and good for keeping my hips from creaking like a barn door. Bone broth makes it taste like Sunday supper, and turmeric keeps me moving without grumbling. You might think these are plain, but to me? They are steakhouse fancy. Hand them over, cowboy, before I start negotiating with the cat.

4.4 Coconut Oat Treats

Old dogs have earned their comfort. These treats are gentle on the belly, easy on the teeth, and carry the kind of simple goodness that does not need fussing. Coconut keeps their coats looking slick, oats settle the stomach, and the whole thing is hearty enough to keep a senior hound satisfied without weighing him down.

Ingredients:

- 2 cups rolled oats
- 1 cup unsweetened shredded coconut
- ½ cup unsweetened applesauce
- 1 egg
- 2 tablespoons coconut oil (melted)
- ¼ cup warm water (add more if needed)

Instructions:

1. Preheat oven to 325°F (160°C) and line a baking sheet with parchment paper.
2. In a mixing bowl, combine oats, shredded coconut, applesauce, egg, and coconut oil.
3. Stir well, adding water a little at a time until dough sticks together but is not soupy.
4. Scoop spoonfuls of dough and press into small round shapes on the baking sheet.
5. Bake 20–25 minutes until edges turn lightly golden.
6. Cool completely before serving so the treats set firm but stay soft inside.

Benefits:

- Oats: Gentle fiber that aids digestion and keeps blood sugar steady.
- Coconut: Adds healthy fats for skin, coat, and brain support.
- Applesauce: Natural sweetness without refined sugar.
- Coconut oil: Extra shine for coats and energy without heaviness.

Gruff's Note

Well, look at this — snacks that taste like a beach vacation without the sand in my fur. Coconut keeps me shiny, oats keep me full, and applesauce makes it sweet enough to trick me into thinking I am getting dessert. Comfort food? You bet. Hand me another before you start bragging about how healthy they are.

Chrissy Hartmann

4.5 Sweet Potato & Ginger Drops

Sweet potatoes are gold for senior dogs—easy to chew, full of goodness, and gentle on their bellies. Toss in ginger, and you have yourself a treat that soothes digestion and settles a sour stomach faster than strong coffee after trail beans. No frills, no tricks—just straight-up nourishment in a bite-sized drop.

Ingredients:

- 1 cup mashed cooked sweet potato, plain, no butter or seasoning
- 2 cups oat flour
- 1 egg
- 2 tablespoons coconut oil
- ½ teaspoon ground ginger
- 1 tablespoon honey, optional, if vet allows
- 2–4 tablespoons water, as needed

Instructions:

1. Preheat oven to 350°F, 175°C, and line a baking sheet with parchment paper.
2. In bowl, mix together sweet potato, egg, coconut oil, ginger, and honey.
3. Stir in oat flour gradually, adding water a little at a time until dough comes together.
4. Drop spoonfuls of dough onto the baking sheet, spacing them a couple inches apart.
5. Flatten lightly with the back of the spoon to help them bake evenly.
6. Bake 20–25 minutes until firm but a little soft in the center.
7. Cool completely before serving to your four-legged senior.

Benefits:

• Sweet Taters: Packed with fiber and beta-carotene for gut and eye health.
• Ginger: Helps ease nausea, bloating, and digestive troubles.
• Oats: Gentle grain that keeps blood sugar steady.
• Coconut oil: Adds healthy fats for brain and coat health.

Gruff's Note

Now this is what I call a belly-fixer. Sweet potato makes it smooth, ginger settles things down when dinner did not agree with me, and the whole drop goes down easy. Tastes good enough I would share with the cat — which I would rather not. So, more for me.

4.6 Low-Fat Chicken Biscuits

Senior dogs cannot be chomping down greasy grub if you want them lasting long on the trail. These biscuits cut the fat but keep the flavor, so your old hound gets his protein without bogging down his belly. It is chicken, flour, and common sense — nothing fancy, nothing foolish.

Ingredients:

- 1 cup cooked chicken breast, finely shredded - plain, no seasoning
- 2-1/3 cups oat flour
- 1 egg
- ½ cup low-sodium chicken broth
- 1 tablespoon olive oil
- 1 tablespoon ground flaxseed
- Water as needed

Instructions:

1. Preheat oven to 350°F, 175°C, and line a baking sheet with parchment paper.
2. In a mixing bowl, stir together chicken, egg, olive oil, flaxseed, and chicken broth.
3. Add oat flour a little at a time, stirring until dough holds together. Add water if dough feels too dry.
4. Roll out dough to about ¼ inch thick.
5. Cut into biscuit shapes and place on baking sheet.
6. Bake 25–30 minutes until golden and firm.
7. Let cool before serving unless you enjoy listening to your dog yelp from a hot mouth.

Benefits:
• Chicken: Lean protein for muscle maintenance without excess fat.
• Flaxseed: Provides fiber and omega-3s for digestion and skin health.
• Olive oil: Keeps joints moving smooth and coats shiny.
• Low-sodium broth: Flavorful without strain on kidneys or heart.

Gruff's Note:
Finally, a biscuit that does not leave me feeling like I swallowed a rock. Lean chicken keeps me strong, flaxseed keeps things moving, and broth makes it tasty enough that I forget it is the healthy kind. Call it low-fat if you want — I call it good eating.

4.7 Glucosamine Mobility Munchers

An old dog's joints creak louder than a bunkhouse door in the wind, and no amount of wishing fixes that. These biscuits are built to keep the gears greased. Glucosamine gives their joints a hand, turmeric fights the fire in their bones, and flaxseed keeps the whole machine running. Feed these to your senior, and he will be moving smoother than you on a payday.

Ingredients:

- 2-1/3 cups oat flour
- ½ cup ground flaxseed
- 1 teaspoon turmeric powder
- ½ teaspoon black pepper
- 1 egg
- ½ cup unsweetened applesauce
- 2 tablespoons olive oil
- ½ cup low-sodium chicken broth
- Glucosamine powder or capsules, vet-approved dosage, usually 500–1000 mg for large dogs, adjust by weight

Instructions:

1. Preheat oven to 350°F, 175°C and line a baking sheet with parchment paper.
2. In a bowl, whisk together egg, applesauce, olive oil, and chicken broth.
3. Stir in glucosamine powder, turmeric, pepper, and flaxseed until blended.
4. Add flour gradually, mixing until a firm dough forms. If too dry, add a splash more broth.
5. Roll dough out to about ¼ inch thick.

6. Cut into bite-sized pieces and place on the baking sheet.
7. Bake 20–25 minutes until golden and firm.
8. Cool completely before serving — dogs with sore hips do not need a burnt tongue added to their troubles.

Benefits:

• Glucosamine: Supports joint cartilage and mobility in aging dogs.
• Turmeric + black pepper: Natural anti-inflammatory to ease stiffness.
• Flaxseed: Fiber and omega-3s for digestion, skin, and joint health.
• Olive oil: Keeps joints moving smoothly and adds healthy fats.
• Oats: Gentle on digestion, easy on sensitive stomachs.

Gruff's Note:

Now you are talking. A biscuit that keeps me running, jumping, and still bossing the yard like a pup. Glucosamine helps me move without sounding like a squeaky wagon wheel, turmeric takes care of the creaks, and flaxseed keeps everything else flowing. Keep them coming, cowboy — I have still got plenty of play left in these paws.

4.8 Salmon Brainy Bites

A senior dog's mind needs feeding same as his belly. Salmon brings the good fats that keep the brain sparking and egg adds protein to back it up. Do not waste time with fancy spices or garnish — this is straight fuel for keeping an old hound clever enough to outsmart you at the supper table.

Ingredients:

- 1 cup canned salmon, plain, packed in water, deboned and drained
- 2-1/3 cups oat flour
- 2 eggs
- 2 tablespoons ground flaxseed
- 2 tablespoons olive oil
- ½ cup low-fat plain yogurt (unsweetened)
- Water as needed

Instructions:

1. Preheat oven to 350°F, 175°C, and line a baking sheet with parchment paper.
2. In a bowl, mash salmon until fine. Stir in eggs, yogurt, flaxseed, and olive oil.
3. Add oat flour slowly, mixing until dough forms. Add a splash of water if too dry.
4. Roll dough out to about ¼ inch thick.
5. Cut into small bite-sized pieces.
6. Place on baking sheet and bake 20–25 minutes until firm but not rock-hard.
7. Cool before serving unless you want a hound howling about a scorched tongue.

Benefits:

• Salmon: Omega-3 fatty acids for brain support, anti-inflammatory effects, and shiny coats.
• Eggs: High-quality protein for muscles, plus choline for brain health.
• Flax Seed: Adds omega-3s and fiber for gut balance.
• Yogurt: Probiotics for digestive health and extra calcium for bones.

Gruff's Note:

Now we are talking smart food. Salmon keeps my brain snapping, eggs keep me strong, and yogurt keeps my belly happy. With treats like these, I will be remembering where every last bone is buried — and probably where you hid the good bacon, too.

4.9 Banana & Hemp Rounds

A senior dog does not need sugar bombs or junk food – he needs steady fuel. Bananas give natural sweetness without riling up the belly, and hemp seeds bring in protein and fatty acids that keep the joints moving and the coat gleaming. These rounds are simple, wholesome, and worth every bite.

Ingredients:

- 2 ripe bananas, mashed
- 2 cups oat flour
- ½ cup unsweetened applesauce
- 2 tablespoons hemp seeds (hulled)
- 1 tablespoon ground flaxseed
- 1 egg
- 2 tablespoons coconut oil
- Water as needed

Instructions:

1. Preheat oven to 325°F, 160°C, and line a baking sheet with parchment paper.
2. Mash bananas smooth in a mixing bowl. Stir in applesauce, egg, and coconut oil.
3. Add flaxseed and hemp seeds, mixing well.
4. Fold in oat flour gradually until dough holds together. Add water if it feels too dry.
5. Scoop spoonfuls of dough and roll into small rounds. Place on baking sheet and press lightly.
6. Bake 20–25 minutes until set and lightly golden.
7. Cool completely before serving to your old pup.

Benefits:

• Bananas: Gentle on the stomach, rich in potassium for muscle and heart health.
• Hemp Seeds: Full of omega fatty acids and protein to support joints, skin, and coat.
• Flax Seed: Fiber and omega-3s for digestion and inflammation support.
• Oats: Easy to digest and steady on blood sugar.

Gruff's Note:

Finally, someone figured out how to make bananas worth eating. Hemp seeds give me the muscle of a younger dog, bananas keep me fueled, and the whole thing goes down smooth. Call them rounds if you want — I call them mine. Keep your hands off my pile, cowboy.

4.10 Golden Delights

Now this here recipe comes straight from the author herself, and it carries some weight. Her old golden lab, Adam, swore by these when he got on in years. They kept him bright-eyed and tail-wagging. I reckon he knew good grub when he tasted it. Carrots bring sweetness and vitamins. Turmeric gives that golden hue and keeps the joints from groaning. The whole mix is plain nourishment for a senior hound.

Ingredients:

- 1 cup grated carrots
- 2-1/3 cups oat flour
- ½ teaspoon turmeric
- ½ teaspoon black pepper
- 1 egg
- ½ cup unsweetened applesauce
- 2 tablespoons olive oil
- 2 tablespoons ground flaxseed
- Water as needed

Instructions:

1. Preheat oven to 350°F, 175°C, and line a baking sheet with parchment paper.
2. In a bowl, mix together carrots, egg, applesauce, olive oil, flaxseed, turmeric, and pepper.
3. Stir in oat flour gradually until dough holds firm. Add water if too dry.
4. Cut dough into small bone shapes.
5. Place on the baking sheet and bake 25–30 minutes until edges turn golden.
6. Let cool completely before serving to your faithful friend.

Benefits:

• Carrots: Rich in beta-carotene for eye health and a natural sweetness dogs enjoy.
• Turmeric + black pepper: Anti-inflammatory duo that supports stiff joints and mobility.
• Flax Seed: Fiber and omega-3s to ease digestion and keep coats soft.
• Olive Oil: Healthy fat that aids skin, coat, and joint lubrication.

Gruff's Note:

Golden Delights, huh? Makes sense—carrots keep me sharp, turmeric keeps me moving, and they shine like treasure in the pan. If Adam loved these, then I am in good company. Now hand me one before I start reminding you that dogs do not share very well.

Author's Thoughts:

Golden Delights
Named after my first guide dog, Adam.

These treats—made with turmeric, carrots, oat flour, flaxseed, egg, olive oil, and grated Golden Delicious apples—were his favorites. Adam was my first Seeing Eye dog, a golden lab with a heart as big as a Texas sky. He was my best friend, my "Buppy," and my shadow through every trail life we traveled.

When I left the house without him, he'd wait by the front steps, head resting on my shoe, patient as ever.

When he got sick with lymphoma, these Golden Delights were about the only thing that soothed his tummy. I made them fresh each day, and every time he took one, he'd give me an extra lick of thanks. I'd lie beside him on the cool laundry-room floor, just keeping him company through the hard nights.

He never left a crumb.

I made sure he had two before crossing the Rainbow Bridge. Maybe they comforted him, maybe they comforted me — either way, they'll always remind me of my golden boy.

A batch of love and memory, baked in honor of my faithful partner, Adam.

Grub Wrangler's Wisdom:

When the saddle's worn, you don't throw out the horse—you just ride gentler. These recipes easy on the teeth and kind to the belly.

The Cowpokes Baking Notes:

Chapter 5 Dog Size Matters

Tiny Tito the Chihuahua once tried to drag a rib bone twice his size. Meanwhile, Big Moose the Great Dane didn't even notice his chew toy was gone.

So, If you don't reckon Dog Size Matters, then you never tried hauling a yapping ankle-biter out of a saloon or wrestling a full-grown hound off your supper plate. That's why we wrangled up a list of the good, the bad, and the doggie pros and cons for ya so you have a good notion of what you're getting into.

5.1 Tiny/Small Dogs

under 20 Pounds

Now listen here, partner. These pint-sized pups may fit in a saddlebag, but don't let their size fool ya. They're feisty little critters, sometimes barking louder than a saloon at high noon. Let's weigh out the good, the bad, and the downright yappy.

Pros:

- Easy to carry, travel with, and fit into small living spaces.
- Generally cheaper to feed, medicate, and groom.
- Long lifespans compared to bigger breeds.
- Easier to handle physically if they misbehave.

Cons:

- Fragile bones and higher risk of injury if mishandled.
- Can be yappy, nervous, or bossy.
- May not do well with small kids or roughhousing.
- Not as intimidating for protection.

5.2 Medium Dogs

20–50 Pounds

Alright, buckaroo. Medium dogs are the middle of the trail—ain't too small to be fragile, ain't too big to crush your boots when they sit on ya. But don't think middling size means middling personality—they can be as wild as a bronco or as steady as a ranch hand.

Pros:

• Good balance between sturdiness and manageability.
• Big enough for outdoor adventures, small enough for apartments (depending on breed).
• Often versatile—many working, sporting, and companion breeds fall here.
• Easier vet bills and food costs compared to large dogs.

Cons:

• May still be too energetic for some households.
• Some breeds shed heavily or need more exercise.
• Not always intimidating enough for guard duty.
• Lifespan shorter than small dogs, though longer than giants

5.3 Large Dogs

50–90 Pounds

Now we're talking, cowboy. These big fellas ain't gonna fit in your saddlebag — they'll need their own wagon. Loyal as a blood brother, but if you don't give them enough room or grub, they'll eat you out of house and home faster than a cattle stampede.

Pros:

• Strong, loyal, and protective—make excellent family guardians.
• Great companions for hiking, running, and outdoor life.
• Often calmer indoors once properly exercised.
• Many breeds excel at working roles (service, rescue, hunting).

Cons:
• Expensive to feed, medicate, and groom.
• Shorter lifespans than small/medium dogs.
• Can accidentally knock over kids or furniture.
• Harder to transport—require more space in cars/homes.

5.4 Extra Large/Giant Dogs

90+ Pounds

Well, partner, here's where things get downright colossal. These hounds are the size of a small horse and eat like one, too. They'll guard your homestead and keep ya warm on a cold prairie night — but blink wrong, and they'll flatten ya like a tumbleweed.

Pros:

- Intimidating presence — few varmints, human or otherwise, will mess with them.
- Gentle giants by nature, often great with kids if raised right.
- Hugging one feels like wrapping your arms around a bear rug.
- Majestic, awe-inspiring companions.

Cons:

- Very short lifespans compared to smaller dogs.
- Extremely high food, medication, and care costs.
- Prone to joint issues and other health problems.
- Require lots of space, and traveling can be a headache.

So, just remember whatever your pleasure is, be it big or small, love them with your whole heart.

Chapter 6 Dog Care Ain't for the Lazy

Now don't go thinking a dog is just a critter that eats scraps and chases rabbits. Nothing burns my biscuits faster than watching folks treat their mutt like he will mend himself if something goes wrong. That's not how it works. A good dog is worth his weight in gold, and if you are not willing to keep him healthy, you don't deserve him.

Gruff – my rascal of a sidekick, keeps me company on the trail, guards the camp, and gives me an ear when no one else will. But let me tell you, he doesn't stay in one piece by accident. Teeth need scrubbing, ears need unclogging, nails need trimming, baths need doing, glands need squeezing. Yeah, we will get to that unpleasant business. And fleas? Lord help me, they will turn a strong hound into a scratching mess if you don't stay on top of it. Vaccinations and vitamins, too – don't think it is fancy talk. A dog needs fuel in the tank and protection against sickness, same as you do.

I will break it down for you, step by step, so you don't foul it up. It isn't glamorous, it isn't quick, and it sure as shooting isn't pretty. But if you stick with it, your dog will thank you – maybe not in words, but in loyalty, which lasts longer than most anything I have known.

6.1: Teeth Worth Smiling Over

Gruff doesn't grin often, but when he does, I'd rather not see a mouth full of yellow barn slats. Dog teeth rot the same as yours if you don't tend them.

Now, don't be thinking you can hand him a rib bone and call it good — half the time bones do more damage than help.

What you need is a dog toothbrush. Yes, they make such things and paste made for canines too. Don't you dare use people paste unless you like poisoning your best friend.

Here's how you do it: start slow, because your hound won't stand still while you poke around in his mouth. Let him sniff the brush first, then rub the gums gently, one side at a time. Daily is best, but if you can't manage that, at least a few times a week keeps rot at bay. And don't skimp on chews — dental treats help scrape off the gunk, but they are no substitute for a proper scrubbing.

Checklist: Teeth Care

[ ] Dog toothbrush
[ ] Dog-safe toothpaste (never human)
[ ] Patience and steady hands
[ ] Dog Dental Wipes
[ ] Dental chews as backup

Brush 3–7 times per week

6.2: Dog Ear Trouble

Now here's a chore most folks forget until their hound starts shaking his head like a busted windmill.

Dog ears collect dirt, wax, and sometimes worse if you leave them be.

Gruff once had a spell where his ears smelled like sour dough gone bad — taught me quick that ignoring ears ain't an option.

Cleaning isn't fancy. Get a dog-safe ear solution from the feed store or vet. Pour a bit in the ear, massage the base until you hear that squishy sound, then step back—your dog will shake like a wet horse. After that, use cotton balls or pads to wipe out the gunk. Never, and I mean never, jam cotton swabs down in there unless you want to pay a vet to fix what you broke.

Do it regularly, especially if your dog's got floppy ears or spends time in the water. Keeps infections from setting in and saves you both a lot of grief.

Checklist: Ear Care

[ ] Dog-safe ear cleaning solution
[ ] Cotton balls or pads (not swabs)
[ ] Towel for the shake-off
[ ] Gentle massage at the ear base

Clean once a month, or weekly for floppy-eared or swimming dogs

6.3: Doggie Unpleasantries

Now, I didn't sign up to be Gruff's rear-end custodian, but life had other plans.

If you ever saw a dog scooting across the floor like he's polishing it with his backside chances are his anal glands are clogged.

I'll spare you the fine details—but they're two little scent sacs that need emptying now and again.

If you're brave (and stubborn as a mule), you can learn to do it yourself with gloves, towels, and a strong stomach. But truth be told, most folks leave this one to the groomer or veteran — and I don't blame them.

Don't ignore it, because left alone it will lead to infections, swelling, and a real sorry dog.

Checklist: Anal Gland Care

[ ] Disposable gloves
[ ] Towels (ones you won't miss)
[ ] Pet-safe wipes for cleanup
[ ] Optional: professional groomer or vet visit

Check every 4–6 weeks, or when scooting happens

6.4: Baths Without a Brawl

Bubbles to Beautify Your Dog

Gruff doesn't love bath time, and I don't either, but it beats riding downwind of a walking manure pile.

Use shampoo made for dogs, not people. Human soap is too harsh and will dry his hide until he scratches himself raw.

And don't make the water too hot or too cold. Lukewarm, like fresh coffee after it's sat five minutes, is just right. Wet him down slow, lather up, and rinse until the water runs clear. No half measures — leftover soap will itch worse than fleas.

Bathing every couple of months is enough for most dogs, unless my Gruff finds something foul to roll in. Then it's straight to the tub, no arguments.

Checklist: Bath Time

[ ] Dog-safe shampoo
[ ] Bucket or handheld sprayer
[ ] Towels (big ones)
[ ] Brush for before and after bath

Bathe every 2–3 months, or as needed

6.5: Nails That Don't Click-Clack

If you've ever heard a dog walking across wood floors sounding like a poker dealer shuffling cards, then you know the nails are too long.

Long nails hurt the paw, split easy, and mess with how a dog walks.

Gruff hates nail trimming worse than bath time, but it has to be done.

You'll need proper clippers, or a grinder made for dogs. Don't grab the rusty wire cutters from your tool chest unless you like accidents.

Trim just the tip, avoiding the quick—that's the tender part with blood vessels. Cut too far and you'll have a bleeding, yelping mess on your hands.

Every three to four weeks is about right, depending on how fast they grow.

Checklist: Nail Care

[ ] Dog nail clippers or grinder
[ ] Styptic powder or baggie of flour (for accidental bleeding)
[ ] Towel to steady the dog
[ ] Rewards or treats from recipes above afterward

Trim every 3–4 weeks 'cause no one likes running on long nails

6.6: Beating Back Fleas and Ticks

Fleas and ticks are freeloaders, plain and simple. They bite, spread sickness, and make a dog miserable.

Gruff once picked up a batch of ticks after running through brush, and I spent half a night picking them out. Never again.

You've got choices: flea collars, spot-on treatments, chewable pills, and sprays. Each has its place, but the point is consistency. Skip a dose or two, and you'll be back to scratching and swatting.

Always check behind ears, between toes, and under the tail—those critters like hiding where you don't look.

Checklist: Flea & Tick Defense

[ ] Flea collar, topical treatment, or chewable (ask vet for best option)
[ ] Fine-toothed flea comb
[ ] Tick remover tool or tweezers
[ ] Regular checks after walks in tall grass or woods

Stick to a monthly prevention schedule

6.7: Vitamins and Good Grub

Feed a dog junk and he'll end up acting like junk.

Gruff runs on quality kibble and sometimes wet food, nothing less. No table scraps — what's good for you might be dangerous for him.

Onions, chocolate, and grapes? Deadly.

Supplements can help if your vet says so — fish oil for the coat, glucosamine for joints, probiotics for the belly. And yes, daily vitamins keep him running strong, just like a cowboy chewing down beans and cornbread needs more than salt.

Fresh water, always. No excuses.

Checklist: Nutrition & Supplements

[ ] Quality dog food (kibble or canned)
[ ] All natural dog biscuits (See Gruff's choices above)
[ ] Fresh water, daily
[ ] Vet-approved multivitamin if needed
[ ] Optional: fish oil, glucosamine, probiotics

No table scraps—ever

6.8: Shots That Keep Trouble Away

Now, Gruff doesn't much care for needles, and truth be told, neither do I. But vaccinations are one of those necessary evils, like boiling coffee so strong it'll strip paint — you may not like it, but it keeps you going.

Skipping shots is asking for heartbreak, plain and simple. Rabies, parvo, distemper—those aren't just big words, they're killers. A healthy-looking dog can go downhill faster than a wagon with no brakes if he's not protected.

Most pups need a series of shots when they're young, then boosters on a regular schedule. Don't think once is enough — you've got to keep up with it, or the protection runs out.

Your vet will lay out the timing, and you'd best stick to it.

I may grumble when I haul Gruff in for his jabs, but I'd rather put up with a few minutes of whining than dig a grave out back.

Checklist: Vaccinations

[ ] Core shots: rabies, parvo, distemper, adenovirus
[ ] Non-core shots (ask your vet): Lyme, Bordetella, leptospirosis, kennel cough, heartworm depending on area

[Puppy series, then adult boosters as scheduled. Keep written records handy. Annual vet visits to stay current. Cause a healthy dog is a good dog.

In closing, Gruff's a Partner Worth the Trouble

I won't lie to you—caring for a dog is work. Some days I gripe about it, same as I gripe about scrubbing pots after supper. But Gruff is my partner. He doesn't complain when the trail gets long, and he doesn't quit when the night gets cold. The least I can do is keep him in one piece. So, roll up your sleeves, do the dirty work, and your dog will give you something rare — loyalty that never wavers... and maybe a big old sloppy kiss too!

Chapter 7: Wrangling Your Hound

Well, pull up a stool and light the lantern, because we've got a lot of ground to cover in this here chapter. You didn't saddle up with a four-legged companion just to let things slide — a dog needs proper care, discipline, and a little bit of respect (whether he's a lap pup or a dirt-track worker). Don't let that swaggering hound run you ragged.

First off: choosing a vet ain't like picking a horse from the herd. You need someone who's steady, trustworthy, and knows their business when it comes to paws and claws. Same with a groomer — don't hand your dog to someone who treats him like a poodle doll unless that's what you want. Find someone who understands a working dog's coat, grit, and the occasional tumble through mud.

Toys might seem frivolous to some, but a bored dog is a mischief machine. A good chew toy or tug rope can save your boots — and your porch boards. And speaking of rules: licensing and insurance ain't just bureaucratic hoops — they're your protection when a dog missteps or a stranger gets too close. Better to have your papers in order before trouble shows up on your doorstep.

Now, working dogs — those hounds meant to chase, guard, herd or hunt — deserve special attention. They're tougher, smarter, and often harder to handle. Make sure their training, workload, rest, and health are all balanced, or you'll have a wild one on your hands.

And behavior issues? Don't you ignore them. A dog that chews, bays, lunges, or ignores your commands is a danger — to himself and to folks around. You don't fix trouble by yelling — you fix it by consistent rules, firm hand, and patience (though I don't promise I'll like doing it).

So, tighten your belt, tip your hat, and let's ride into the next section — you'll walk away knowing how to pick pros, protect your pup, and keep that dog behaving like the best darn hound in the territory

.

7.1: Picking a Vet

Now, I've patched up plenty of cowboys with whiskey and a rag, but when it comes to Gruff, I leave the doctoring to someone with letters after their name.

Picking the right vet ain't something you do blindfolded. You wouldn't trust your best horse to a shifty blacksmith, so don't hand your dog over to the first fella with a stethoscope and a half-off coupon.

A good vet clinic ought to look clean, smell halfway decent, and run with folks who treat your dog like more than a number. Watch how they handle Gruff—or any dog—that'll tell you everything.

If they grab him rough or talk down to me like I'm too thick to follow directions, I turn on my heel and take my business elsewhere.

Wellness checks are like trail inspections before a long ride. They might seem like wasted time, but they catch the busted nails, ear infections, and belly bugs before they turn into trouble. The vet checks Gruff's heart, lungs, teeth, weight, and all them things I can't fix with a skillet and common sense. Costs a little, saves a lot.

Vaccines and treatments fall under the same roof. Rabies ain't just a law—it's life or death. Distemper, parvo, and the rest of those fancy-named plagues are nothing to gamble on. I keep Gruff current on his shots and flea, tick, and heartworm preventatives.

He may pout about the needles or the pills, but I'd rather deal with a sulking dog than a sick one.

Checklist: Vet Care

[ ] Visit once a year for wellness check
[ ] Watch how the vet and staff handle your dog
[ ] Make sure clinic is clean and professional
[ ] Stay up to date on vaccinations (rabies, distemper, Bordetella ,parvo, etc.)
[ ] Ask about preventatives for fleas, ticks, and heartworms
[ ] Keep written records for future reference

When you lasso the doc with the golden stethoscope , make sure the pup sees him at least once a year.

7.2 Groomers and Bubbles

Now, Gruff don't need a top hat or a bow tie, but a good groomer keeps him from looking like a dust-covered tumbleweed. Picking the right one is as important as picking the right vet—because a rough-handed groomer can leave your dog scared, scratched, or worse.

Look for a groomer who knows what they are doing. Check the place for cleanliness and organization. Watch how they handle dogs. If they're calm, patient, and talk to your dog like he's a living, breathing partner instead of a raggedy mop, you've probably found a keeper.

Services should cover more than a simple haircut. Baths, ear cleaning, nail trimming, anal gland attention, and brushing are part of the job. If they skip one or two of these and charge full price, walk out and don't look back.

Some dogs need special care — long coats, curly coats, or sensitive skin—so ask what they're used to handling.

And don't overlook the red flags: hair left tangled, dogs left in cages too long, staff acting frazzled or rough. You wouldn't ride a horse that hadn't been groomed; don't let your dog suffer the same fate.

Checklist: Groomer Care

[ ] Check for cleanliness, proper equipment, and calm environment
[ ] Watch how staff handle other dogs before leaving yours
[ ] Ensure services cover bathing, brushing, nail trimming, ear care, and glands
[ ] Ask about experience with your dog's coat type or special needs
[ ] Avoid groomers who rush or handle dogs roughly

If you take kindly to a day at the spa, then I reckon your pup would to. Book ahead of time, most A+ groomers don't have many spur of the moment openings.

7.3 Paperwork Nobody Likes

Now, I'll be honest—paperwork ain't exactly how I planned to spend my days on the trail. But licensing your dog and keeping him properly identified is one of them chores you just can't skip.

It keeps Gruff legal, and it keeps him from disappearing into someone else's pasture or worse.

Licensing is the law in most towns, plain and simple. You pay your fee, get a tag, and you've got proof your dog belongs to you.

Put that tag on the collar where it can't get lost. Include your name, phone number, and city. That way, if he wanders off chasing a rabbit, folks know exactly who to call.

Trackers are another layer of safety. Microchips are tiny, painless, and permanent—you only need a scanner to find him. Tattoos work too, but microchips are faster and easier if he gets picked up by animal control.

Doesn't matter if your dog is a lazy couch potato or a four-legged trail hound, identification is insurance for both of you.

Checklist: Licensing & Identification

[ ] Obtain city or county dog license
[ ] Attach tag to collar
[ ] Include owner name and phone number,
[ ] Consider microchip for permanent tracking
[ ] Optional: tattoo for extra backup

Keep all paperwork current and in an accessible place

Chrissy Hartmann

7.4: When You Can't Be There

Sometimes, even a hard-working cowboy like me can't be everywhere Gruff needs to be. That's when a good dog walker or daycare comes in handy — but only if you pick the right one. Don't just let any Tom, Dick, or Sally take your hound for a stroll or stash him in a cage.

For walkers who come to your home, look for reliability and experience. They should know how to handle your dog on a leash, watch for hazards, and follow feeding or medication instructions if needed.

Ask for references, meet them in person, and see how your dog reacts. If he hides in the corner, that's a warning bell.

Kennel-based daycares have a different set of checks. Cleanliness, proper fencing, secure gates, and safe ratios of dogs to staff are non-negotiable.

Watch how the staff interacts with the dogs. Are the dogs happy, or are they barking and pacing like cattle in a squeeze chute?

Make sure they have procedures for medical emergencies, accidents, and escapes.

Either way, the key is supervision, safety, and clear communication. Your dog should come home tired but happy, not stressed or injured. And remember, puppies, seniors, or working dogs may have extra needs — don't assume a one-size-fits all approach works.

Checklist: Daycare & Dog Walkers

[ ] Meet the walker or daycare before committing
[ ] Check cleanliness, fencing, and safety measures
[ ] Ask about staff-to-dog ratios and supervision practices
[ ] Confirm they follow feeding, medication, or special care instructions
[ ] Watch for your dog's reaction—happy, relaxed, and well-exercised is the goal

Make sure your pooch gets the blue ribbon of treatment and keep them rodeo clowns at bay.

Chrissy Hartmann

7.5: Toys for the Nippers to Chewers

Don't go thinking toys are just for pampered pooches. Gruff may be a rugged trail dog, but a good toy keeps him occupied, healthy, and out of trouble.

Size matters. A Chihuahua doesn't need a giant rubber bone made for a Mastiff, and a Great Dane will laugh at your puny squeaky mouse.

• Chew toys help keep teeth strong and jaws busy.
• Puzzle toys challenge his brain.
• Fetch toys burn off energy.
• Tug toys teach manners if your dog knows the rules.
• Soft plushies can comfort younger pups or senior dogs.

Always inspect toys before giving them to your dog.

• Splintered wood, torn fabric, or tiny parts that can be swallowed turn fun into danger faster than a horse spooks at lightning.
• Rotate toys to keep them interesting and avoid boredom.

Checklist: Dog Toys

[ ] Select size-appropriate toys for your dog's breed and strength
[ ] Include chew toys, puzzle toys, fetch toys, and tug toys
[ ] Inspect regularly for damage or hazards
[ ] Rotate toys to keep interest high
[ ] Avoid small pieces that can be swallowed

Picking the right one ain't guesswork. It's about size, durability, and safety.

7.6: Because Trouble Costs Money

Now, I don't like paying for anything I can't taste or ride, but dog insurance is one of them rare things that actually saves you money when trouble hits.

Gruff is sturdy, but accidents happen, illnesses crop up, and vet bills pile faster than firewood in winter.

Dog insurance can cover accidents, illnesses, and sometimes even wellness checks and vaccinations.

Some plans pay a percentage, some have a fixed payout – read the fine print like your life depends on it, because it just might if your dog swallows something he shouldn't.

Factors to consider: deductibles, coverage limits, exclusions, and monthly premiums.

Don't just grab the cheapest plan; make sure it actually helps when your dog breaks a leg, eats a skunk, or contracts something nasty.

Paying a little now beats shelling out hundreds or thousands–later.

Checklist: Dog Insurance

[ ] Compare coverage for accidents, illnesses, and optional wellness care
[ ] Check deductibles, payout limits, and exclusions
[ ] Choose a plan that fits your dog's age, breed, and health history
[ ] Keep insurance documents accessible and updated

Review annually to make sure coverage still fits your needs

7.7: Wild Pup to a Good Partner

Listen here, a dog without training is like a campfire with no wood — messy, unpredictable, and liable to burn you if you're not careful.

Gruff didn't learn manners by magic. Nope, he sure didn't. In fact, it took time, patience, and a whole lot of grumbling.

Basic obedience—sit, stay, come, heel—is non-negotiable. A dog that ignores you is a danger on a leash and a nuisance at home.

Use consistent commands, treats, and praise when he does right.

Don't yell, don't scare, just be firm and clear. Dogs catch on quicker than most folks think if you stay steady.

Socialization is just as important. Introduce your dog to different people, other dogs, noises, and environments early. Puppies are like sponges; adults can learn, but it takes a little extra grit.

If your household has cats, don't throw them together and hope for the best. Start slow: let them sniff each other through a gate or crate, reward calm behavior, and gradually allow supervised visits. Keep sessions short and positive so neither critter feels cornered.

Proper socialization keeps your dog confident, less anxious, and prevents nasty habits from forming.

If you hit a wall, don't be ashamed to call a pro trainer.

Sometimes a stubborn dog like Gruff needs someone with extra patience and know-how. Better that than letting him grow into a cantankerous outlaw who refuses to obey anyone.

Checklist: Training & Socialization

[ ] Teach basic commands: sit, stay, come, heel
[ ] Use consistent commands, treats, and praise
[ ] Introduce new people, dogs, cats, and environments gradually
[ ] Start cat introductions slow, through barriers, supervised, and reward calm behavior
[ ] Attend puppy classes or training sessions if possible

Seek professional help for stubborn or behavioral issues.

7.8: Not All Dogs Work the Same Job

Now don't go thinking every dog is cut from the same cloth.

Gruff's a trail-hardened companion, but some dogs pull weight in ways most folks never see.

Working dogs aren't just pets—they're partners with jobs that demand focus, training, and care beyond the average tail-wagger.

- Guide dogs help folks see the world safely.
- Therapy dogs bring comfort to hospitals, schools, and nursing homes.
- Emotional support dogs calm anxiety and stress for their humans.
- Police and military K9s track scents, find drugs or explosives, and sometimes protect lives on the line.

Each type of working dog needs more structured training, consistent routines, and special attention to their health and mental well-being.

Even if your dog isn't "on duty," understanding what makes a working dog tick teaches patience and respect. They thrive on structure, tasks, and mental stimulation. A household pet may not need full harness work, but providing challenges, exercise, and training keeps them sharp and happy. Recognize your dog's strengths and tendencies, and you'll have a partner who's reliable, safe, and downright loyal — just like Gruff.

Checklist: Working Dog Awareness

[ ] Understand your dog's role: pet, guide, therapy, emotional support, or police/military
[ ] Provide extra training, structure, and mental stimulation for working dogs
[ ] Maintain regular vet checks, nutrition, and fitness routines
[ ] Respect boundaries and task-specific needs
[ ] Recognize signs of stress, overwork, or boredom

The Grub Wrangler's Wisdom:

I'll be straight with you – keeping a dog healthy, happy, and out of mischief ain't for the lazy or faint-hearted.

Gruff doesn't just roll out of bed ready to be perfect. I reckon that would be mighty fine, but in all reality, he needs vets, groomers, proper ID, toys, training, and even mental work to keep from turning into a four-legged outlaw. And that's just the start.

Some dogs carry heavier loads—guide dogs, therapy dogs, police K9s—they demand more attention, more patience, and more know-how.

It's a lot of chores, sure. You'll scrub, sweep, scrub some more, and double-check everything twice. You'll grumble about the vet bills, the insurance premiums, and the extra work. But here's the truth: do it right, and your dog gives you something rare. Loyalty that never wavers, companionship that steadies the worst days, and a friendship worth every scraped knuckle and grumbled word.

So, keep the teeth clean, the nails short, the ears smelling decent, the shots up to date, and the toys entertaining. Keep training, socializing, and giving your dog purpose — even if it's just guarding the porch or keeping you company by the campfire. Do all that, and your dog will stick closer than your shadow.

Gruff's lived it, I've lived it, and I can tell you: the work is worth every bit of dirt, sweat, and grumble along the way.

Thanks, all for listening.

The Cowpokes Pet Care Notes:

Chrissy Hartmann

Chapter 8 Trails End

When the trail finally runs out, and our dogs — like my Daisy, Adam, Maddie, Winnie, and my cats, Boomer, Spencer, and Brutus — lay down their paws for the last time, it sure carves a hole in the heart big enough to drive a chuckwagon through.

Funny thing though — dog spelled backwards is God, and maybe that's no accident. No critter teaches us loyalty, patience, or unconditional love quite like they do, and that's why they'll always be man's best friend.

So, when it's their turn to head on ahead, I like to picture them waiting for us at the Rainbow Bridge: tails wagging, eyes shining, whole bodies wriggling with joy until the day we meet again and finish the ride together.

Until then, give them love, a good place to rest, and lots of these here biscuits... They'll know it all comes from your heart!

And remember, a good dog is worth their weight in gold. Feed 'em right, treat 'em fair, and they'll guard your heart till the cows come home.

— The Grub Wrangler

The Rainbow Bridge
by William N. Britton, 1994
By the edge of a woods, at the foot of a hill,
is a lush, green meadow where time stands still.
Where the friends of man and woman do run,
when their time on earth is over and done.
For here, between this world and the next,
is a place where each beloved creature finds rest.
On this golden land, they wait and they play,
till the Rainbow Bridge they cross one day.
No more do they suffer, in pain or in sadness,
for here they are whole, their lives filled with gladness.
Their limbs are restored, their health renewed,
their bodies have healed, with strength imbued.
They romp through the grass with nary a care,
until one day they stop and suddenly stare.
For there, at the bridge, your figure they see,
their eyes full of joy, and eager with glee.
With a leap of pure love, they run once more,
and stand by your side to part nevermore.
Then together you cross, united and free—
the Rainbow Bridge into eternity.

Chapter 9 Miss Kitty's Feline Treats

Miss Kitty never barked, but she sure hollered if her tuna biscuits ran out.

Well, boy howdy! Here's a bonus chapter for those of you who have one of them their fluffy felines that like to tag along with the chuckwagon.

From Kitten, Prime, and Senior Cat Needs these are some favorites your mouser won't hesitate to thank you for.

Here's a few things to keep in mind for those vittles for the cats to keep them healthy so they can keep those varmints from hosting their own dinner party in your chuckwagon.

Kitten:

- High protein
- Soft texture

Prime:

- Balance of moisture
- Taurine
- Protein

Senior:

- Easy-to-digest
- low-phosphorus
- Hydration-friendly

Now keep on following this here trail if you got one of them felines that would love to have some healthy all natural treats of their own. Dog's might be this grub wrangler's best friend, but them there kittens are pretty purrfect companions when all's quiet here on the ranch and the cowboys are tending to the herd. And hey, it's nice to have someone to grumble to once and a while.

9.1 Tuna & Egg Soft Bits

Now here's a treat fit for every stage of a barn cat's life, from those rowdy little kittens clear up to the old-timers snoozin on the porch rail. Tuna & Egg Soft Bits come together quick, with honest ingredients you can feel good about slipping to your four-legged ranch hands. Soft, hearty, and packed with protein, these little bites aim to keep whiskers twitching and tails high no matter the age.

Ingredients

- 1 can tuna in water, drained
- 1 large egg, lightly beaten
- 2 tbsp oat flour (or finely ground oats)
- 1 tsp olive oil (optional, for shine and softness)
- 1 tbsp water (if dough is too dry)

Instructions

1. Preheat oven to 350°F (175°C) and line a baking sheet with parchment paper.
2. In a bowl, mash the tuna until smooth.
3. Add the beaten egg and mix thoroughly.
4. Stir in oat flour until a soft dough forms. If too dry, add water a little at a time.
5. Roll small pea-sized portions and place them on the baking sheet.
6. Bake for 8–10 minutes, just until set but still soft.
7. Allow to cool completely before serving. Store in the fridge for up to 5 days.

Benefits:

• For Kittens: Soft enough for teething mouths and stacked with protein to help those little rascals grow strong.
• For Prime-Time Cats: Keeps muscles sturdy and energy burning for prowling, pouncing, and raising mischief.
• For Seniors: Easy on the teeth and rich with omega-3s to keep the joints greased and the mind sharp as a cactus spine.

Miss Kitty's Opinion:

Well, sugar, these bites meet my standards — moist, tasty, and downright regal. But don't you dare think about passing my portion to that barn cat next door. A lady of my stature deserves the whole batch.

Chrissy Hartmann

9.2 Chicken Liver Nibblets

If you've ever had a barn cat trailing you close, chances are good they've caught the scent of chicken livers. Chicken Liver Niblets are a hearty, wholesome treat that'll win favor with the spry kittens, the prime hunters, and the old porch loungers alike. They're simple to whip up, rich in flavor, and pack the kind of nutrition that keeps whiskers perky at any age.

Ingredients

- 1 cup chicken livers (cooked and finely chopped)
- 1 egg (lightly beaten)
- 2 tbsp oat flour (or finely ground oats)
- 1 tbsp parsley (optional, chopped fine)
- 1 tbsp water (if dough needs loosening)

Instructions

1. Preheat oven to 350°F (175°C) and line a baking sheet with parchment paper.
2. Chop the cooked chicken livers into tiny bits and place them in a bowl.
3. Stir in the beaten egg until well blended.
4. Mix in oat flour and parsley, working the mixture into a soft dough.
5. Roll small marble-sized pieces and set them on the baking sheet.
6. Bake for 10–12 minutes, until firm but still tender.
7. Cool completely before serving. Store in the fridge up to 5 days.

Benefits:

- For Kittens: Rich in iron and B vitamins to fuel growth and play, with a texture soft enough for teething mouths.
- For Prime-Time Cats: Delivers protein to keep muscles limber and hunters ready to spring into action.
- For Seniors: Easy on the teeth, full of nutrients that keep coats shiny as a polished saddle, and gentle on the belly.

Miss Kitty's Opinion:

Well, well... finally a cook who understands refinement. These morsels are rich, savory, and practically melt on the tongue. Just be warned, sugar — I expect them served on a china saucer, not a barn tin.

9.3 Pumpkin Puree Cookies

Come fall on the ranch, even the barn cats perk up when pumpkins roll out of the wagon. Pumpkin Puree Cookies are a soft, belly-friendly treat made to suit every stage of a cat's trail—whether it's a kitten learning the ropes, a prime-time prowler keeping watch, or a wise old senior napper soaking in the sun. Gentle, hearty, and downright wholesome, these little cookies will keep tails swishing and paws tapping for more.

Ingredients

- ½ cup plain pumpkin puree (not pie filling)
- 1 egg (lightly beaten)
- ½ cup oat flour
- 1 tsp dried catnip (optional, for a little mischief)
- 1 tbsp water, if dough feels too stiff

Instructions

1. Preheat oven to 350°F (175°C) and line a baking sheet with parchment paper.
2. Stir together pumpkin puree and the beaten egg until smooth.
3. Mix in oat flour and catnip, working until dough comes together.
4. Roll into tiny balls or flatten into small cookie shapes on the baking sheet.
5. Bake for 10–12 minutes, until just set but still tender.
6. Let cool before serving. Store leftovers in the fridge up to 5 days.

Benefits

• For Kittens: Easy-to-chew with pumpkin that's gentle on small tummies and fiber to keep digestion running smooth.

• For Prime-Time Cats: Light yet filling, with vitamins that help keep eyes sharp and muscles ready for nightly barn patrol.

• For Seniors: Soft on teeth, packed with fiber to settle slower bellies, and full of nutrients that support healthy aging.

Miss Kitty's Opinion:

Pumpkin? Normally I leave vegetables to the rabbits, but these little cookies are soft, fragrant, and surprisingly elegant. Please keep them coming in steady supply.

9.4 Catnip Cheese Treats

Now here's a recipe that'll get whiskers twitching before the oven door even shuts. Catnip Cheese Treats blend the sharp bite of cheddar with a sprinkle of mischief, making a snack fit for kittens with energy to burn, prime-time hunters stalking their turf, and seniors lounging in the afternoon sun. One whiff and you'll have a four-legged shadow following you from the kitchen to the corral.

Ingredients

- ½ cup shredded cheddar cheese (low-sodium if possible)
- 1 egg (lightly beaten)
- ½ cup oat flour (or finely- ground oats)
- 1–2 tsp dried catnip- 1 tbsp water, if dough needs softening

Instructions

1. Preheat oven to 350°F (175°C) and line a baking sheet with parchment paper.
2. In a bowl, stir together cheese and beaten egg.
3. Add oat flour and catnip, mixing until dough holds together.
4. Roll into small balls.
5. Bake for 8–10 minutes, until firm on the outside but soft inside.
6. Cool before serving. Store in the fridge up to 5 days.

Benefits

• For Kittens: A playful mix of flavor with protein to fuel all that wild climbing and pouncing.
• For Prime-Time Cats: Keeps muscles steady and spirits lively, with catnip that brings out their inner ranch rascal.
• For Seniors: Soft enough for tender mouths, rich with protein, and enough catnip to create a gentle spark.

Miss Kitty's Opinion:

Cheese and catnip? Now you're speaking my language. These treats strike the perfect balance between indulgence and entertainment. Just know, if you leave the bag unattended, I might stage a full-scale raid.

Chrissy Hartmann

9.5 Sardine Softies

If there's one smell that'll have a cat strutting into the kitchen quicker than you can holler "supper," it's sardines. These here sardine softies are tender, savory morsels brimming with flavor that suits every age of feline, from the bright-eyed kitten to the seasoned porch sentinel. Packed with healthy oils and plenty of protein, these bites are as close to a barnyard delicacy as you'll find for your whiskered companions.

Ingredients

- 1 can sardines in water, boneless
- 1 egg, lightly beaten
- ½ cup oat flour
- 1 tsp olive oil, optional, for extra softness
- 1 tbsp water, as needed if dough feels too stiff

Instructions

1. Preheat oven to 350°F (175°C) and line baking sheet with parchment paper.
2. Drain sardines, blend smooth.
3. Stir in beaten egg and olive oil.
4. Add oat flour and mix until dough forms.
5. Roll into small balls.
6. Bake for 8–10 minutes, until just firm.
7. Cool before serving. Store in the fridge up to 5 days.

Benefits

• For Kittens: Gentle texture and omega-3 fatty acids to support growing brains and shiny coats.
• For Prime-Time Cats: High-protein fuel for prowling, leaping, and claiming every sunny spot in the house.
• For Seniors: Soft enough for delicate mouths, with fish oils that soothe joints and keep coats sleek as polished leather.

Miss Kitty's Opinion:

Finally—a recipe worthy of my refined palate. Sardines are the very definition of luxury. Serve me these Softies on a silver tray, and I might just grace you with an extra purr... emphasis on might.

Grub Wrangler's Wisdom:

Even though I ride with dogs, I tip my hat to the cats too. These are feline-approved. And to be honest, them felines are always howling for more, especially them there little ones.

The Cowpokes Baking Notes:

Howdy Partner,

Just wanted to thank you for reading this here dog biscuit almanac. I hope you find the book as entertaining as it was to lasso it all together.

I've had a number of years to rustle up these here recipes. My golden lab, Adam loved the Golden Delights the best. Winnie? Well, never found one she didn't like.

And as for the kitten treats, my official-taste testers, Brutus and Punkin never had a lick of trouble with any of these.

Again, thank you kindly for taking the time to check this cookbook out. I love my dogs and cats and just wanted to create something to keep them healthy. In turn, I hope it provides some tasty treats for your pup and kitten too.

I'd love to hear from you. I welcome all comments, photographs, and better yet would love a review. You can leave a review on the store's website from where you purchased this gem or better yet, leave one on Good Reads.

And don't hesitate to send me a telegram about your best fur-legged friend. I'd love to mention your story in my monthly newsletter, the Prickle Forrest Chronicles. You can send it via chrissyhartmann@sssnet.com

From tip to tail, the Grub Wrangler and I thank you from the bottom of our hearts,

Chrissy Hartmann

Chrissy Hartmann

About Chrissy Hartmann ...

Chrissy Hartmann's a Buckeye born and bred – raised on her grandparents' horse farm and dodging Lake Erie waves like a pro. She writes romances that stick to your ribs, edits, reviews, and occasionally dabbles in poetry when the mood strikes – but don't expect it to rhyme.

She's been wrangling animals longer than most folks have been breathing—one first dog as a kid, another as an adult, and two guide dogs, and enough kittens over 55 years to start a feline rodeo. That obsession led to this here dog Biscuit Cookbook, The Grub Wrangler and Gruff: Dog Biscuit Almanac because apparently, telling tails isn't enough – she had to bake them too.

When she's not making words or biscuits fly, she's sipping coffee like it's moonshine, spinning vinyl with her hubby, bossing her Eagle Scout around, or stealing snuggles from her furry gang. Cozy coffee shops, indie bookstores, and libraries make her heart do a little two-step, and grapeseed oil is her sidekick in the kitchen – healthy, handy, and occasionally used as lasso bait.

Her stories? Full of heart, soul, and just enough grit to remind you this cowboy ain't soft. Hop on her social media trail at USAWriter355 or ride on over to www.ChrissyHartmann.com

Chrissy's Booklist

All Chrissy's books can be found on her website: https://chrissyhartmann.com/books

Cookbooks

- *The Grub Wrangler and Gruff: Dog Biscuit Almanac*
- *The Grub Wrangler: Heartfelt Grapeseed Oil Recipes with Benefits*

Whiskey Salvation Series

- *Rescuing Whiskey's Salvation*
- *Cherishing Whiskey's Salvation: A Whiskey Salvation Novella*
- *Treasuring Whiskey's Salvation* (Coming Soon)
- Merry Christmas Whiskey: A Whiskey Salvation Christmas Novella

Anthologies

- *Buckeye Hearts and Lone Star Kisses (coming 2026)*
- *Holidays in the Heartland: Ohio Christmas Tales*
- *Tales from the Prickle Forrest*
- *Love on the Lakefront: Romantic Tales from the Great Lakes*

Short Stories

- *Make Christmas Great Again*

Photography Acknowledgments

Cover Photo

The Grub Wrangler and Gruff: Dog Biscuit Almanac – Design by Getcovers

Recipe Photography

• Golden Delight Biscuits – Photography by Jacob Benchoff

• Pumpkin and Peanut Biscuits – photography by Jacob Benchoff

• Parsley Mint Biscuits – photography by Jacob Benchoff

•Blueberry Soft Chews – photography by Jacob Benchoff

• Bone Broth Biscuits – photography by Jacob Benchoff

• Biscuit package display photography by Jacob Benchoff

• Pet care package basket photography by Jacob Benchoff

Family and Friends' Contributions

A heartfelt thanks to the following family and friends for generously sharing their photos:

• Calico kitty - Cupcake sitting on deck rail looking up – Photo credit to owner Cary Harter

• Brown and Black Labradoodles – Sawyer and Mayer wearing bandanas in snow – Photo credit to owners Erica and Cyndi Boyer

• Brown labradoodle – Mayer puppy – Photo credit to owner Erica Boyer

• Shepherd mix - Storm sitting on floor with pink bandana photo credit to owner Seth Wallace

• Rusty- border collie photo credit to owners Edward and Kelly Hartmann

• Ginger – Border collie photo credit to owners Edward and Kelly Hartmann

• Ginger/Rusty border collie lying in leaves and sticks photo credit to owners Edward and Kelly Hartmann

• Ginger and Rusty border collies with paws crossed photo credit to owners Edward and Kelly Hartmann

• German Shepherd - Capo Canton Fire Department Arson Unit with service medals – photo credit to handler and owner Joe Carafelli

• German Shepherd - Capo and Joe riding on motorcycle photo credit to owner Joe Carafelli

• American Leopard Hound, Saidie on Walking trail photos credit to owner Brady Hartmann

• Yorkie - Ralphie in green harness – Photo credit to owner Renee Mack

• Yorkie – Tank sitting on red plaid blanket – Photo credits to owners Ed and Rebecca Hartmann

• The HartFelt Boarding Kennels – photograph credit to Mary Hartmann

• Siberian Huskey in doorway – photograph credit to Mary Hartmann and the HartFelt Boarding Kennel

• German Shepherd in play yard – photograph credit to Mary Hartmann and the HartFelt Boarding Kennel

• Rottie Bathtime bubbles – photograph credit to Mary Hartmann and the HartFelt Boarding Kennel

• Shih Tzu with cowboy hat and bandana – photograph credit to Mary Hartmann and the HartFelt Boarding Kennel

• Mary and three dogs on couch – photograph credit to Mary Hartmann and the HartFelt Boarding Kennel

• German shepherd puppy in playroom – photograph credit to The Seeing Eye

• "Kiser" puppy photograph credit to Cary Harter from permission of the puppy's owner Michelle McCrock

• Junie with pink ball in mouth photograph credit to owner Drew Paul

• Bandit cat with green eyes photograph credit to owner Alexandra Musselman

• German shepherd watching goat photo credit to the dog and goat's owner, Deb gray

• Payzlee a cream-colored poodle puppy looking up at the camera – photograph credit to owner Zondra Hershberger

• Grizzley Bernese Mountain dog playing in snow photography credits to owner Heidi Hardin Meshew

• Giant schnauzer , Holly wearing blue bandana photography credit to owners Jack and Becky Papp

• Colli Bassett Hound mix, Brody, walking in snow photography credit to owner Julie Ann Dawson

• Doberman pincher, Mia Mae, wearing pink spike collar photography credits to owner Shannon Metzo Bennett

• Maci in pink sweater photography credits to owner Patricia Hasapis

• Pup, Tucker, standing on couch photography credits to owner Teresa Ann Powell

Stock Images

All stock images licensed from PixABay.com, used with permission.

• PurpleFlowersAndKeesheand-dog-7991199 - Photographer Credits to: JackieLou DL

• Merle-6WeekOldPuppy-8510899 - Photographer credits to brixiv

• Lab Puppy looking up 3071334 - Photographer credits to moshehar

• Chocolate lab-puppy-looking up – 5447540 Photographer credits to ameliausmoothie

• Pink Sunglasses-Pink Bowtie-Pink Background- pug-8632718 - Photographer credits to HelpingHounds

• Brown labrador Portrait-5762115 Photographer CREDITS TO RebeccasPictures Rebecca Schultz

• Puppy-BrownLabCatchingTreats-dog-5021242 Photographer CREDITS TO Felix Wolf

• Bernese Mountain Dog in cherry blossoms-guvo59-bernese-mountain-dog-7928156 Photographer credits to Gundula Vogel

• Bernese Mountain-puppy-1284673 Photographer credits to AngelaAnaconda

• GreatDanePuppy-ButterflyChair-dog-2871914 Photographer credits to SarahRichterArt

• Snowflakes-australian-shepherd-5902421 Photographer credits to RebeccasPictures - Rebecca Sholz

• AustralianShepherd-Running-Snow-dog-5773397 Photographer credits to Wolfgang157- Wolfgang Herath

• HappyHour-Water-food-bowl-430347 Photographer credits to TaniaVdB - Tania Van den Berghen

• Pumpkin-in-Patch-8278499 Photographer credits to debannja - Debrah Jackson

• Saint Bernard - Goat - 6773771- Photographer credit to pangrea

• Old dog-golden retriever- park -5663220 Photographer credit to taylorarisa

• Dog-food- bowl – paws -5168940 Photograph credit to mattycoulton

- Puppy-bath - 1022421 - Photographer credit to mandaCullingford

- Dog nail-clipping-6926857 Photographer credit to Alektas

- dachshund with balloons around him celebrating his birthday photographer credits to RebaSpike – StarFleetPets

Special Thanks...

To all the adorable canine taste testers and photography contributors who made this book visually delightful!

Prickle Forrest Books

Established in 2023, Prickle Forrest Books LLC was created due to the stigma attached to self-published and indie authors. Prickle Forrest Books took up the call to help promote these fabulously talented authors to the readers of the world. By doing this, they have provided an affordable service to get the word out. Prickle Forrest Books loves all authors, but Indie and self-published take priority. Prickle Forrest Books hopes one day all authors can publish on a level page. We wish all authors the greatest success in their writing careers. Thank you for letting us help you reach your dreams.

For more information on our publishing services, visit our website, https://prickleforrestbooks.com or contact us: prickleforrestllc@sssnet.com.

Index

www.ingramcontent.com/pod-product-compliance
Lightning Source LLC
Chambersburg PA
CBHW040844120626
46547CB00001B/15

* 9 7 8 1 9 6 5 7 8 0 1 1 4 *